Macmil
English
Book
4

ry Bowen
Louis Fidge
Liz Hocking
Wendy Wren

MACMILLAN

Unit 1

Comprehension

1 **Read Language Book 4, pages 8–9 again.**

2 **Put the sentences in order.**

______ The Wind says he can make trees fall over and clouds move.

___1___ The Wind and the Sun are arguing.

______ The Sun shines and the Man takes off his coat.

______ The Cloud sees the Man walking in the valley.

______ The Wind says he is stronger than the Sun.

______ The Sun says he can make the grass burn and the water dry up.

______ The Wind blows but the Man holds on to his coat.

______ The Sun says he is stronger than the Wind.

Vocabulary

You can make words from the letters in other words.

yes ← yesterday → stay

day ← yesterday → date

1 Make two words from the letters in each of these words.

1 walking → king / → ______

2 reading → ______ / → ______

3 holding → ______ / → ______

4 arguing → ______ / → ______

2 Add letters to these words to make longer words.

1 ring bring bringing

2 wing ______ ______

3 lean ______ ______

4 tick ______ ______

Language building

Remember! A **noun** is a naming word.
A **proper noun** starts with a capital letter.
An **adjective** is a describing word.

1 Underline the nouns. Circle the proper nouns.

1 tree	2 Tilly	3 water	4 January
5 coat	6 Friday	7 Professor Inkspot	8 hat

2 Write five nouns.

____
____
____
____
____

3 Write five proper nouns.

____
____
____
____
____

4 Sort out these colour adjectives.

1 d e r ___red___ 2 e g n r e __________
3 l e b u __________ 4 a e n o r g __________
5 l o w e l y __________

5 Write an adjective to describe each of these.

1 ___pretty___ flower 2 __________ snow
3 __________ meal 4 __________ boy
5 __________ teacher 6 __________ ball

Grammar

1 Complete the sentences. Choose from these verbs. Use the past tense.

go get catch blow

1 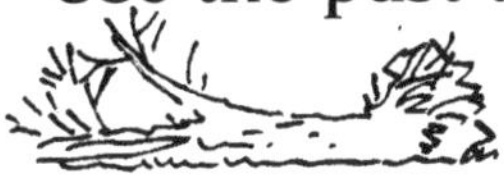 The wind ____________________ a tree over.

2  The boy ____________________ the ball.

3  The children ____________________ to school by bus.

4  She ____________________ a kitten for her birthday.

2 Correct the sentences. Use *did not*.

1  The boy saw a plane. ____________________

2  The girl heard a cat. ____________________

3  The tree fell down. ____________________

4  Mum made a cake. ____________________

3 Write Tom' questions.

1 Anna bought some new shoes.

What ____________________

2 Bill and Ben went to Australia.

Where ____________________

3 Uncle Bob came here to see us.

Why ____________________

4 Joe ate six slices of pizza.

How many ____________________

4 Look at the pictures. Answer the questions.

1 Did Joe go to the window or the door?
2 Did he look at the sky or along the road? What did he see?
3 Did the car come closer in a cloud of smoke or a cloud of dust?
4 Did the car stop outside the supermarket or Joe's building?
5 Did a man or a woman get out?
6 What did she have? Who was it?

5 Write the story.

Spelling

Remember! The letters **ey** at the end of some words make the sound **ee**.

1 Label the pictures. Use the words in the box.

chimn**ey**	monk**ey**	turk**ey**	jock**ey**

1 

____

2 

____

3 

____

4 

____

2 Write sentences using these *ey* words.

1 

money ____

____

2 

honey ____

____

3 

donkey ____

____

Writing

The Man with the heavy coat and the Woman with the hat have a conversation.

- The Man tells the Woman:
  He was walking in the valley.
  The wind blew very hard.
  He held on to his coat.
  The sun shone.
  He got very hot.
  He took off his coat.
- The Woman tells the Man:
  She was walking in the valley.
  The wind blew.
  The sun shone.

1 What do you think happened next?
Did the wind blow the Woman's hat off?
Did the sun make the Woman take her hat off?
Write your answer here.

2 Write the scene in your own words.

Man

Woman

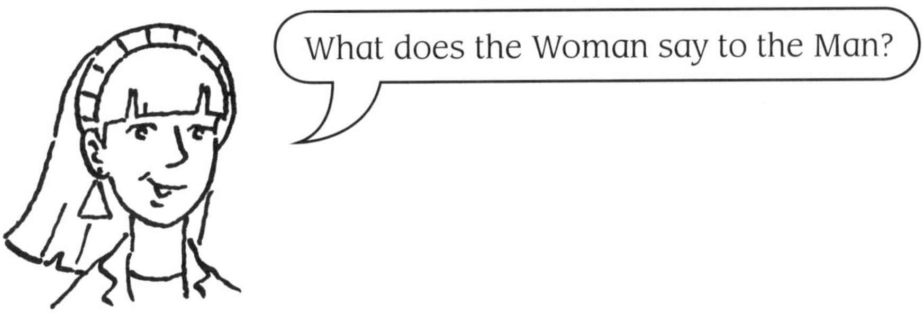

Unit 2

Comprehension

1 **Read Language Book 4, pages 16–17 again.**

2 **Match the beginning of each sentence with the correct ending.**

1 Mountains take millions of years	c	**a**	fire, smoke and lava.
2 Volcanoes can grow	____	**b**	deep inside the Earth.
3 Long ago there were	____	**c**	to grow big.
4 They poured out	____	**d**	it is called lava.
5 Volcanoes start to grow when	____	**e**	in a few weeks.
6 Magma moves up from	____	**f**	there is a deep crack in the earth.
7 Magma pours out	____	**g**	thousands of volcanoes.
8 When magma pours out	____	**h**	of the crack.

Vocabulary

1 **Complete the crossword.**

Clues across →

5 a mountain which can grow in a few weeks

6 explode

Clues down ↓

1 hot, liquid rock inside the Earth

2 a 'sleeping' volcano is this

3 the hole in the top of a volcano

4 hot, liquid rock flowing out of a volcano

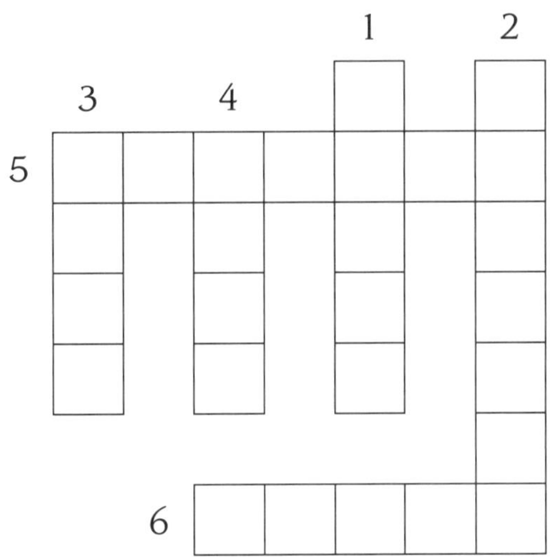

2 **Put the words you have written in the crossword in alphabetical order.**

1 ______________ 2 ______________

3 ______________ 4 ______________

5 ______________ 6 ______________

Language building

Remember! '**Singular**' means 'one'.
'**Plural**' means 'more than one'.
Many nouns make their plural by adding **s** or **es**.

1 **Complete the crossword. Write the plurals.**

Clues down ↓

1  one piano two ____________

2  one volcano two ____________

3  one tomato two ____________

Clues across →

4  one potato two ____________

5  one cello two ____________

6  one hero two ____________

Grammar

1 **Tom and Katie went to the zoo last week. What was happening? Complete the sentences. Use these verbs:**

ride feed sleep eat swim

1 The monkeys were eating bananas.
2 A boy ______
3 The lion ______
4 The penguins ______
5 The girl ______ the elephant.

2 **Make questions using these words.**

1 lion roar — Was the lion roaring?
2 camel run ______
3 penguins swim ______
4 elephant sleep ______

3 **Answer the questions. Use *not*.**

1 Was the lion roaring? The lion was not roaring.
2 Was the boy riding an elephant? ______
3 Were the monkeys eating apples? ______
4 Was the girl feeding the camel? ______

4 Look at the picture. Answer the questions.

1 What was the weather like?
2 Was the wind blowing the trees?
3 Were people walking slowly or hurrying along the street? What were some of them carrying?
4 Were a woman and a girl standing in the rain or under a tree? What were they waiting for?
5 Was a boy standing under the tree or was he jumping in the puddles? Did he like the rain?

5 Write about the picture.

A rainy afternoon

Spelling

1 Write the words. Read the words you make.

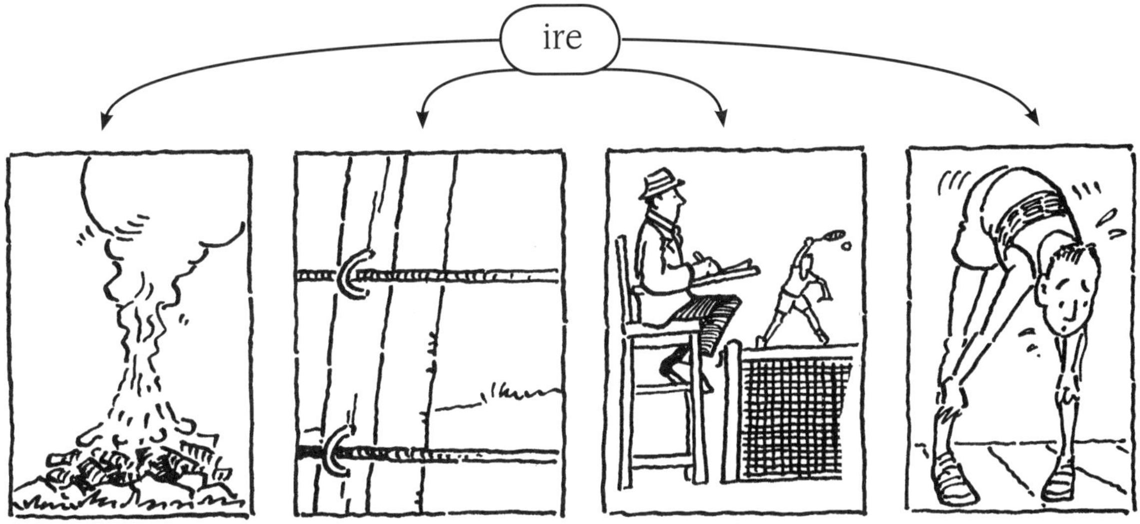

1 fire 2 ________ 3 ________ 4 ________

2 Choose the correct word from the box.

fire	wire	umpire	tired

1 something you find in a computer ________
2 sleepy ________
3 something that keeps us warm ________
4 referee ________

3 Use these *ire* words in sentences of your own.

1 wire ____

____

2 fire ____

____

Writing

1 **Match the questions about Etna with their answers.**

1 Where is Mount Etna?	c	a The nearby town is called Catania.
2 How high is Mount Etna?	_____	b Mount Etna first erupted in 476 BC.
3 When did Mount Etna first erupt?	_____	c Mount Etna is in Sicily.
4 What is the name of the nearby town?	_____	d Lava and ash have covered the nearby town twice.
5 How many times have lava and ash covered the nearby town?	_____	e Mount Etna is 3263 metres high.

2 **Match the questions about Vesuvius with their answers.**

1 Where is Mount Vesuvius?	_____	a Mount Vesuvius erupted in AD 79.
2 How high is Mount Vesuvius?	_____	b Pliny wrote about Mount Vesuvius.
3 When did Mount Vesuvius erupt?	_____	c Mount Vesuvius covered Pompeii and Herculaneum in lava and ash.
4 Which towns did Mount Vesuvius cover in lava and ash?	_____	d Mount Vesuvius is in Italy.
5 Who wrote about Mount Vesuvius?	_____	e Mount Vesuvius is 1220 metres high.

3 Write about the volcanoes.

1 Write about Mount Etna.

2 Write about Mount Vesuvius.

Unit 3

Comprehension

1 **Read Language Book 4, pages 24–25 again.**

2 **Choose the correct answer.**

1 Polly answered the door for the first time. She saw ___c___

a her sister **b** a dog **c** a wolf

2 He had come to ________

a eat Polly **b** cook for Polly **c** bring Polly some toffee

3 Polly made ________

a a pie **b** a chocolate cake **c** toffee

4 The wolf had ________

a one piece **b** two pieces **c** three pieces

5 Polly answered the door for the second time.
She made ________

a a pie **b** a chocolate cake **c** toffee

6 The wolf had ________

a two slices **b** four slices **c** six slices

7 Polly answered the door for the third time. She made ________

a a pie **b** a chocolate cake **c** toffee

8 The wolf burned ________

a his hand **b** his nose **c** his mouth

Vocabulary

Remember! **Homophones** are words which sound the same but are spelled differently.

1 Write the homophones. The clues will help you.

Word	Clue	Homophone
1 know	the opposite of *yes*	____________
2 too	a number	____________
3 write	the opposite of *left*	____________
4 sea	you do this with your eyes	____________
5 so	you do this with a needle	____________
6 knew	the opposite of *old*	____________
7 be	an insect	____________
8 beech	a sandy place	____________

2 Write sentences using 4 pairs of homophones from activity 1.

1 ____

____

2 ____

____

3 ____

____

4 ____

____

Language building

Remember! In **direct speech** we write the exact words someone said. We put **speech marks " "** at the beginning and at the end of the spoken words.

1 **Write what they said. Use speech marks. Say who was speaking.**

1 

"Hello, Polly. I've come to eat you!" said the wolf.

2 

____

3 

____

4 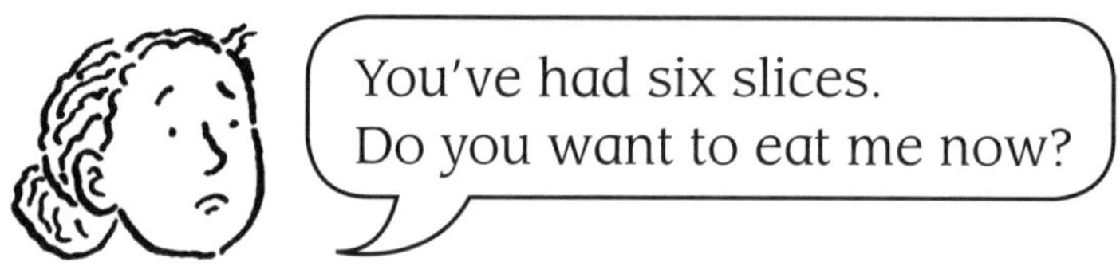

____

5 

____

Grammar

1 Look at the pictures and complete the sentences. Use the verbs in the box.

see ring start find

1 

While she was washing the dishes, ______________________________

2 

While they were playing football, ______________________________

3 

______________________________ while he was working in the garden.

4 

______________________________ while they were swimming.

2 Complete the sentences with the verbs. Be careful! Put each verb into the correct past tense.

1 (climb, break)

While he ________________ the tree, a branch ________________ .

2 (hear, walk)

We ________________ wolves while we ________________ in the hills.

3 (sleep, come)

While you ________________ , your friends ________________ here.

4 (break, wash)

I ________________ a glass while I ________________ the dishes.

3 **Look at the pictures.**
Answer the questions.

1 What happened while Kati was washing clothes in the river?
Was she happy or sad?

2 What was there in the river? What did the fish see? What did it do?

3 What happened the next day while Hans was fishing in the river?

4 Where did he take the fish?

5 What did Kati do with the fish?

6 What did they find while they were eating the fish?
Was Kati happy or sad?

4 **Write the story. Give it a title.**

Spelling

1 Find the *le* words for these pictures in the wordsearch. Circle them.

1 

2 

3 

4 

5 

6 

a	c	a	n	d	l	e	d	r	y
n	t	s	u	u	l	h	p	a	o
e	j	s	w	n	r	q	g	t	w
e	o	c	r	a	d	l	e	t	u
d	r	a	v	s	d	k	z	l	t
l	q	s	x	a	a	f	b	e	l
e	d	e	f	k	e	t	t	l	e
c	b	h	y	y	e	g	f	x	k
t	r	i	a	n	g	l	e	t	i
a	x	m	k	r	k	g	s	a	b

2 Write the words.

1 ____________ 2 ____________

3 ____________ 4 ____________

5 ____________ 6 ____________

Writing

The wolf came to see Polly again!
What happened?

1 Answer the questions.

1 What did Polly bake?

cake

pie

pizza

Polly baked a __________ .

2 Polly opened the door. What did the wolf say to Polly?

3 What did Polly say to the wolf?

4 What did the wolf eat?

____

____

5 Polly asked the wolf:

Are you going to eat me now?

6 What did the wolf say?

2 What happened when the wolf came to see Polly again? Write what they said. Use speech marks.

Unit 4

Comprehension

1 **Read Language Book 4, pages 32–33 again.**

2 **Answer the questions.**

1 How many starters are on the menu? __________

2 How many main courses are on the menu? __________

3 Which vegetables can you have with your main course?

____

4 How many desserts are on the menu? __________

3 **Read Language Book 4, pages 32–33 again.**

4 **Answer the questions.**

1 How much butter do you need for the recipe? __________

2 How much cheese do you need for the recipe? __________

3 Which three things do you do with the potatoes?

____

____

____

4 Which two things do you sprinkle on the potatoes?

____

____

Vocabulary

We can group words together if they all link up to the same subject.

grass	flower	tree

1 Underline the odd one out in each group.

1	pizza	sun	cake	melon
2	cloud	wind	sea	snow
3	lava	magma	vent	week
4	dress	toffee	shoe	hat
5	eyes	mouth	hand	nose
6	tree	car	van	lorry
7	run	fly	jump	walk
8	red	blue	flower	green

2 Complete the word webs.

sister ________

family

________ ________

apple ________

food

________ ________

3 Make your own word web.

________________ ________________

________________ ________________

Language building

Remember!
The names of places like restaurants are **proper nouns**.
A proper noun starts with a **capital letter**.
The words in a book title usually start with capital letters.

1 **This is your restaurant. Think of a name for it. Write the name in the space.**

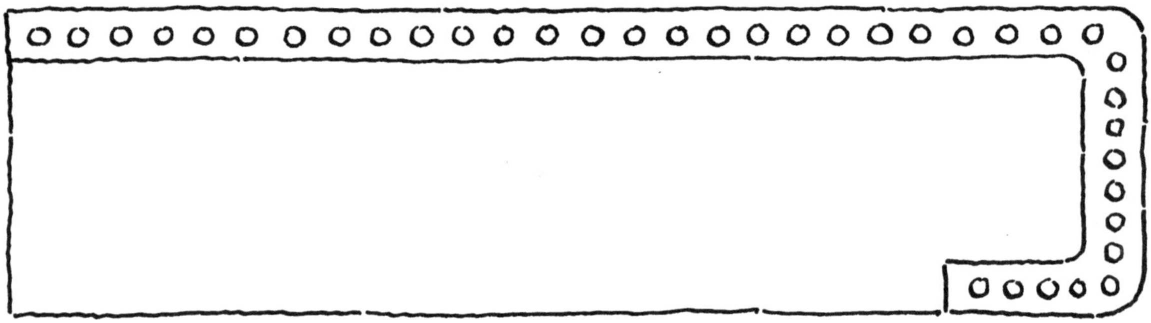

2 **Write these book titles. Put capital letters in the correct places.**

1 island adventure

2 professor inkspot's garden

3 computer games

3 **Write:**

1 the title of a book you like.

____

2 the name of your favourite shop.

____

Grammar

1 Complete the sentences using the words in the box.

to learn	to make	to buy
to celebrate	to put	to play

1 Mum went to the market ______________________ some fruit.
2 She bought some fruit ______________________ a fruit salad.
3 She bought some cream ______________________ on the fruit salad.
4 Tom went to the sports club ______________________ basketball.
5 Lucy went to France ______________________ French.
6 The family had a lovely meal ______________________ Harry's birthday.

2 Answer the questions.

1 Why did Ben and Sue go to the zoo?

They went to the zoo to see the monkeys.

2 Why did they go to the circus?

____

3 Why did Mum go to the baker's?

____

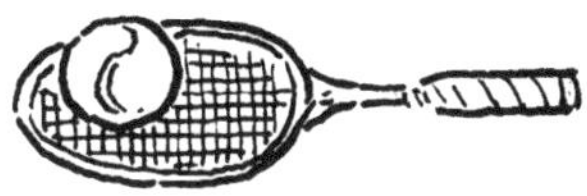

4 Why did Jenny go to the sports club?

____

5 Why did Dad stay at home?

____

6 Why did Tom buy a camera?

____

3 Look and read.

Sami and Darius were fishermen. One day while they were fishing, there was a terrible storm and their boat sank. They swam to a nearby island. This is what happened next.

4 Answer the questions.

1 Why did Sami and Darius cut down trees?

2 Why did Sami climb a palm tree?

3 Where did they sit during the day? Why?

4 What did they light at night? Why?

5 In the morning, what did the sailors on a passing ship see?

6 Where did they row? Why?

5 Write the story.

Spelling

1 Match the words and the pictures. Write the words.

1 j**ar** 

2 c**ar** 

3 st**ar** 

4 sc**ar** 

______ ______ ______ ______

2 Choose the correct word. Write the word.

1 A (c**ar** / st**ar**) has four wheels. ______

2 We can see a (sc**ar** / st**ar**) in the sky. ______

3 We keep jam in a (j**ar** / c**ar**). ______

4 The man has a (c**ar** / sc**ar**) on his arm. ______

3 Write the *ar* words.

arch **ar**my coll**ar** b**ar**k

1 ______

2 ______

3 ______

4 ______

Writing

Harry is making strawberries with ice cream and chocolate sauce.

1 These are the things he needs. Label the pictures.

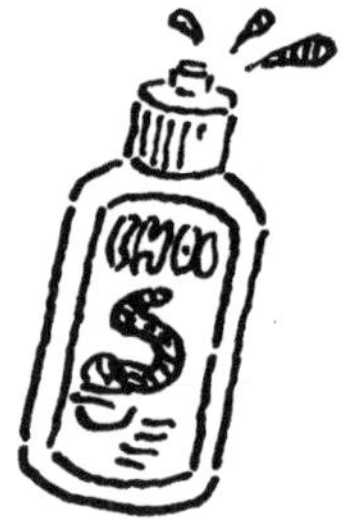

1 ________________ 2 ________________ 3 ________________

2 These are the things he does.

1

wash water

2

scoop bowl

3

tip strawberries

4

shake bottle

5

squeeze sauce

6

eat spoon

3 Write the instructions for making strawberries with ice cream and chocolate sauce.

You need: ______________________________

____

____

Instructions:

Step 1

____

____

Step 2

____

____

Step 3

____

____

Step 4

____

____

Step 5

____

____

Step 6

____

____

Check-up 1

1 Complete the sentences using the verbs in the box. Use the past tense.

take	eat	come	cut
get	run	make	fall

1 My grandparents ____________ to stay last week.

2 They ____________ me and Ben to the park.

3 Ben ____________ along a path.

4 He ____________ over and ____________ his knee.

5 When we ____________ home, Grandma ____________ a chocolate cake.

6 Ben ____________ three slices.

2 Correct these sentences. Use *did not*.

1 

The sun shone all day.

____

2 

He put his hat on the table.

____

3 

The wind blew the house down.

____

4 

She rang the bell.

____

5 

They went to town by bus.

____

3 **Complete the sentences with the verbs.**
Be careful! Put each verb into the correct past tense.

1 (climb, see)

While he was climbing in the mountains, he ____saw____ an eagle.

2 (start, have)

It ________________ to rain while we ________________ our picnic.

3 (ring, eat)

Someone ____________ the doorbell while they ____________ dinner.

4 (cook, burn)

While she ________________ , Polly ________________ a saucepan.

5 (watch, come)

While we ________________ television, Dad ________________ home.

6 (arrive, do)

Uncle Joe ________________ , while I ________________ my homework.

4 **Answer the questions.**

1 Why did Lucy go to the market?

She went to the market to buy some flowers.

2 Why did Meg and her mother go shopping?

____

3 Why did Henry climb the tree?

____

4 Why did Polly phone home?

____

5 Why did the boys stay at school?

____

Unit 5

Comprehension

1 **Read Language Book 4, pages 42–43 again.**

2 **Put the sentences in order.**

_____ They rested at the top of the hill.
_____ They reached the big tar road.
_____ Naledi showed the letter to the driver.
__1__ Tiro and Naledi left the village.
_____ Naledi began to sing.
_____ The driver asked them where they were going.
_____ Tiro wished they had money for the train.
_____ The driver took them to Jo'burg.
_____ Tiro wanted to stop and eat.
_____ A lorry stopped.

Vocabulary

Remember! **Adjectives** tell us more about nouns. **Adjectives** describe nouns.

1 Choose the best adjective to go with each noun.

delicious	round	large	tiny
yellow	~~beautiful~~	strong	green

1 beautiful flower
2 ______ pizza
3 ______ elephant
4 ______ grass
5 ______ ant
6 ______ wind
7 ______ ball
8 ______ sun

2 Put the adjectives in alphabetical order.

1 ______
2 ______
3 ______
4 ______
5 ______
6 ______
7 ______
8 ______

3 Find the opposite of each word. Write the letter.

1 hot c
2 big ______
3 open ______
4 short ______

a closed
b long
c cold
d little

Language building

1 Complete the table with *walk* or *walks*.

Singular	Plural
I ________	we ________
you ________	you ________
he ________	they ________
she ________	
it ________	

2 Complete each sentence with *is* or *are*.

1 The children ________ very hungry.
2 The driver ________ in the lorry.
3 Her legs ________ tired.
4 We ________ nearly there.
5 Their mother ________ surprised.
6 Grandmother ________ worried.

3 Complete each sentence with *He* or *They*.

1 ________ drives a big lorry.
2 ________ sit on the grass.
3 ________ drink some water.
4 ________ wants to stop.
5 ________ sings as he walks.
6 ________ ride in the lorry.

Grammar

1 Complete each sentence with *should* or *should not*.

1 Lisa's hair is a mess. She ______________________________ brush it.

2 Grandma is sleeping. You ______________________________ make a noise.

3 Tom looks very tired. He ______________________________ go to bed late.

4 We are in the library. We ______________________________ talk quietly.

5 The boys ______________________________ play football in the house.

6 If you are thirsty, you ______________________________ drink some water.

2 Write a sentence for each picture. Use *should* or *shouldn't*. The words in the boxes will help you.

see	write	wear
wash	go	eat

doctor	ice creams	bed
hat	wall	face

1  He should wash his face.

2 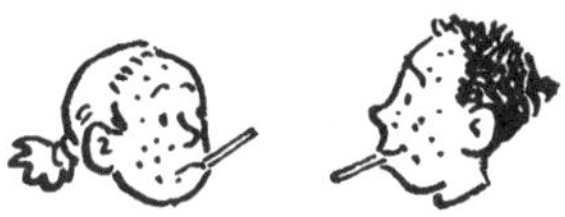 They ______________________________

3  She ______________________________

4  You ______________________________

5  He ______________________________

6  She ______________________________

3 Look and read.

There is a new boy at school. The other children in the class are giving him some advice.

4 Write.

School rules

You should

You should not

Spelling

1 Complete the crossword.

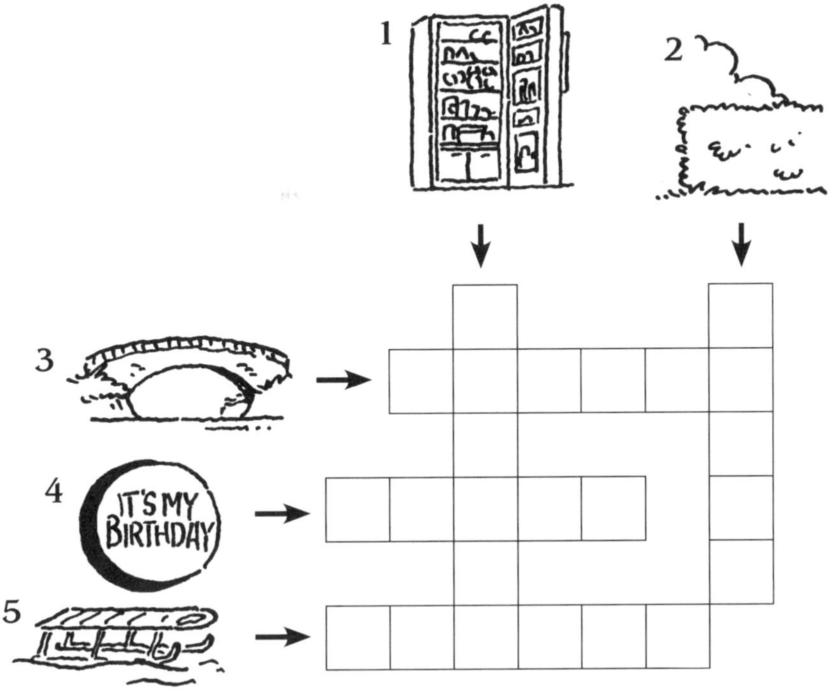

2 Write sentences using these *dge* words.

1 he**dge** ____________________

2 ba**dge** ____________________

3 sle**dge** ____________________

4 bri**dge** ____________________

Writing

1

happy grumpy funny sad kind unkind frightening helpful

Choose words to describe Mr Brown. Write the words you have chosen.

____

____

2 Answer the questions.

1 Is Mr Brown tall or short? ______________________

2 Is Mr Brown young or old? ______________________

3 Is Mr Brown fat or thin? ______________________

4 What colour are Mr Brown's eyes? ______________________

5 What colour is Mr Brown's hair? ______________________

3 Now write more about Mr Brown.

1 What sort of person is he?

2 What does he look like?

Unit 6

Comprehension

1 **Read Language Book 4, pages 50–51 again.**

2 **Choose the correct answer.**

1 Kim wrote a letter to _______

a Amy **b** Katy **c** her mother

2 The plane left at _______

a 6.30 am **b** 8.00 am **c** 10.30 am

3 Amy couldn't close her suitcase because _______

a it was old **b** it was too full **c** it was broken

4 Before they left, Dad _______

a made lists **b** drove the taxi **c** watered the plants

5 At the airport they waited for _______

a 20 minutes **b** two hours **c** five hours

6 On the plane, Kim _______

a had something to eat and drink **b** went to sleep **c** read a book

7 They were on the plane for _______

a 20 minutes **b** two hours **c** five hours

8 When they plane landed they were met by _______

a Katy **b** their family **c** their friends

Vocabulary

A	B	C	D	E	F	G	H	I	J	K	L
1	2	3	4	5	6	7	8	9	10	11	12
M	N	O	P	Q	R	S	T	U	V	W	X
13	14	15	16	17	18	19	20	21	22	23	24
Y	Z										
25	26										

1 Crack the code. Write the words.

23 5 ______

18 5 1 4 ______

1 ______

16 12 1 25 ______

3 1 12 12 5 4 ______

20 8 5 ‘______

19 21 14 ______

1 14 4 ______

20 8 5 ______

23 9 14 4 ______’.

2 Write your name in code.

______ ______

3 Write your friend's name in code.

______ ______

Language building

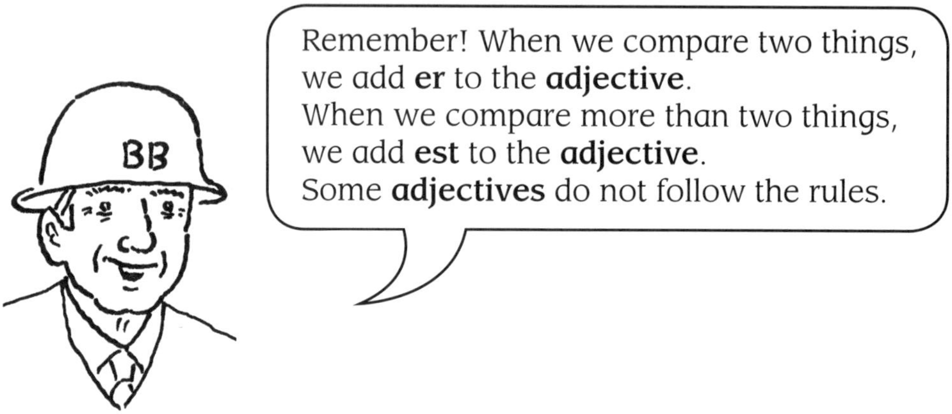

1 **Add *er* to the adjective to complete each sentence.**

1 This journey is (long) ________________ than the last one.
2 Today is (warm)________________ than yesterday.
3 It is (cold) ________________ outside than inside.
4 The grass here is (green)________________ than over there.
5 My brother is (young) ________________ than I am.

2 **Add *est* to the adjective to complete each sentence.**

1 There are three mountains. This is the (high) ________________ .
2 There are five dogs. This is the (small) ________________ .
3 I have two brothers. I am the (tall) ________________ .
I am the (old) ________________ .
Sam is the (young) ________________ .

3 **Complete the chart.**

Adjective	Comparing two things	Comparing more than two things
good	better	the best
bad	________________	the ________________
many	________________	the ________________

Grammar

1 What will the children do tomorrow?
Complete the sentences using the verbs in the box.

visit	buy	help	do	play	go

1 Sally ______________________ to the supermarket with her mother.
2 They ______________________ fruit and vegetables.
3 Bill and Ben ______________________ basketball at the sports club.
4 Lenny ______________________ his father in the garden.
5 Susie ______________________ her grandmother.
6 Dan and Lizzie ______________________ their homework.

2 Write questions to match the answers.

1 How old ______________________
on Sunday? Jenny will be twelve.
2 What ______________________
She'll have a party.
3 Who ______________________
She'll invite her friends.
4 What ______________________
They'll bring presents.
5 Will ______________________ Yes, there'll be a cake.
6 How many ______________________ It will have twelve candles.

3 Answer these questions about Jenny. Use *not*.
1 Will Jenny be eleven on Sunday? ______________________
2 Will she have an exam? ______________________
3 Will her cake have ten candles? ______________________

4 Look at this weather map of Coconut Island. This is what the weather will be like next week.

5 Answer the questions.

1 Where will it be hot?
2 Where will it be cool?
3 Where will it be very cold?
4 Where will it be wet?
5 Where will it be sunny?
6 Where will it be windy?
7 Where will it be cloudy?
8 Where will it snow?

6 Write the weather forecast for Coconut Island.

In the north ____________________

____

In the south ____________________

____

In the west ____________________

____

In the east ____________________

____

In the mountains ____________________

____

Spelling

The **g** in each of these words sounds like **j**.

1 Sort the words.

1

i n t g a

____

2

r g o n a e

____

3

r a f e f g i

____

4

s e v e l b g a e t

____

2 Choose a word from the box to complete each sentence.

messa**g**e　　**g**emstone　　en**g**ine　　gara**g**e

1 We put the car in the ____________________ .

2 I got an e-mail ____________________ on my computer.

3 This piece of jewellery has got a big ____________________ .

4 The car's ____________________ has stopped.

Writing

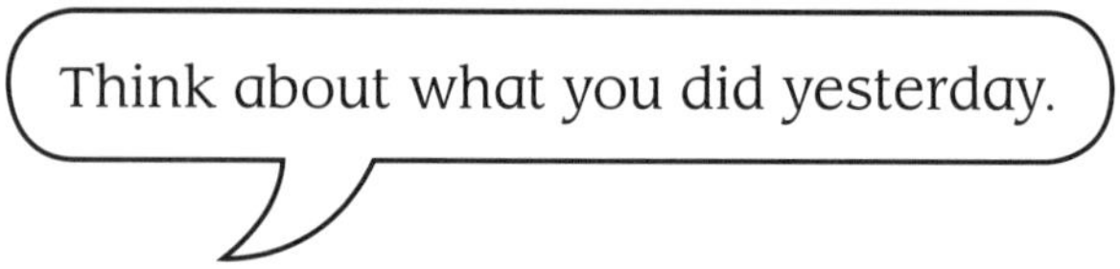

1 Answer the questions.

1 What time did you get up? ______________________________

2 What did you have for breakfast? ______________________________

3 What time did you go to school? ______________________________

4 What did you do in the morning? ______________________________

5 What did you have for lunch? ______________________________

6 What did you do in the afternoon? ______________________________

7 What did you have for tea? ______________________________

8 What homework did you have? ______________________________

9 What did you do in the evening? ______________________________

10 What did you like doing best?

____

____

____

____

11 What did you like doing least?

____

____

____

____

2 Write a letter to your friend. Tell your friend what you did today.

Write your address here.

Write your friend's name here.

Write about what you did before you went to school here.

Write about what you did in the morning here.

Write about what you did in the afternoon here.

Write about what you did in the evening here.

Sign off here.

Unit 7

Comprehension

1 **Read Language Book 4, pages 58–59 again.**

2 **Match the sentences with the pictures.**

1 He was very lazy.
2 He was collecting grain.
3 He liked to sit in the sunshine.
4 He did no work.
5 He got food for the winter.
6 He came out of his nest.
7 He had no food.
8 He always worked in the summer.

Sentence numbers

_____ _____

_____ _____

Sentence numbers

_____ _____

_____ _____

Vocabulary

Remember! Words with similar meanings are called **synonyms**.

1 Match the pairs of words with similar meanings. Write the letters.w

1	closed	e	a	tiny
2	noise	____	b	large
3	small	____	c	sleepy
4	quick	____	d	cold
5	pretty	____	e	shut
6	tired	____	f	beautiful
7	cool	____	g	sound
8	big	____	h	fast

2 Replace each underlined word with a synonym.

1 The ant was small. The ant was tiny.

2 The beetle was always tired.

____

3 The beetle shut his eyes.

____

4 The weather was very cool.

____

5 The ant heard a noise outside the nest.

____

Language building

1 Copy the table. Fill in the missing adjectives.

Adjective	Comparing two things	Comparing more than two things
beautiful	more beautiful	most beautiful
delicious	_____ __________	_____ __________
terrible	_____ __________	_____ __________
surprising	_____ __________	_____ __________
comfortable	_____ __________	_____ __________

2 Write sentences using these adjectives.

1 more frightening

____

____

2 most important

____

____

3 more useful

____

____

Grammar

1 Complete each sentence with a word from the box.

something anything nothing

1 Is there ______________ in your pocket?

2 No, I've got ______________ in my pocket.

3 Look! I can see ______________ in that tree.

2 Complete each sentence with a word from the box.

somebody anybody nobody

1 Listen! There's ______________ at the door.

2 Has ______________ got my pen?

3 No, ______________ has got your pen.

3 Complete the sentences. Use words from the box.

something anything nothing
somebody anybody nobody

1  There is ______________

2  I can see ______________

3  I'm thirsty. Is there ______________

4  My pencil's broken. Can ______________

5  Look! There's ______________

6  The doorbell rang but there is ______________

4 Look at the pictures.

Look! There's something in the tree.

There isn't anything in the box.

Come here, Katie. We've got something for you.

I can't see anything under the table.

5 Answer the questions. The speech bubbles will help you.

1 Who did Mum call into the garden? What did she say?

2 What was on the garden table? What did Katie do? What did she say?

3 What did Mum do? What did she say?

4 Where did Dad point? What did he say? What was in the tree?

6 Write the story.

A surprise for Katie

Spelling

1 Write the silent letters in these words.

1 knife silent k

2 write silent ____

3 kneel silent ____

2 Add the missing silent letter *k* or *w*.

1

_ n i t

2

_ r o n g

3

_ r a p

4

_ n o w

5

_ n e e

6

_ r i s t

Writing

1 **Look at the pictures. Read the words. Answer the questions.**

A

sunny ant beetle food

B

hid tree

C

looked round

D

ran shouted

E

asleep leaves

F

cross woke up

1 What do you think the ant shouted in picture **D**?

"____ ," shouted the ant.

2 What do you think the ant said in picture **F**?

"____ ," said the ant.

3 What do you think the beetle said in picture **F**?

"____ ," said the beetle.

2 Now write the story.

Beginning (Pictures A and B)

Middle (Pictures C and D)

Ending (Pictures E and F)

Unit 8

Comprehension

1. Read Language Book 4, pages 66–67 again.

2. Complete the chart.
Find three mammals. Describe them.

Animal	Description

3. Complete the chart.
Find three animals that live in water. Describe them.

Animal	Description

Vocabulary

1 Write each animal's name in the correct space.

kangaroo	hawk	squirrel	moose	
elephant	yak	fox	zebra	~~bear~~
jackal	python	vole	rabbit	newt

1 ant	2 bear	3 cheetah	4 dog
5 ________	6 ________	7 giraffe	8 ________
9 ibis	10 ________	11 ________	12 leopard
13 ________	14 ________	15 orang-utan	16 ________
17 queen bee	18 ________	19 ________	20 tiger
21 unicorn	22 ________	23 walrus	24 x-ray fish
25 ________	26 ________		

Language building

Remember! A **possessive noun** tells you who owns something.
It has an **apostrophe '** and an **s** at the end.

1 Match. Write the letters.

1 the tail belonging to the dog ___c___
2 the ears belonging to the rabbit ______
3 the horn belonging to the unicorn ______
4 the fur belonging to the bear ______
5 the pouch belonging to the kangaroo ______

a the unicorn's horn
b the kangaroo's pouch
c the dog's tail
d the rabbit's ears
e the bear's fur

2 Underline the owner in each of these.

1 the cat's whiskers
2 the dog's paw
3 the newt's tail
4 the yak's horns
5 the zebra's stripes
6 the giraffe's neck

3 Write sentences using these possessive nouns.

1 lamb's

____

2 python's

____

3 fox's

____

Grammar

1 Complete each sentence with *little* or *few*.

1 There are ________________ tigers in the wild.

2 There is ________________ water in the river.

3 ________________ food grows in the desert.

4 ________________ eagles live in the mountains.

2 Complete each sentence with *less* or *fewer*.

1 I have got ______________ money than you.

2 You have got ______________ books than me.

3 In this country there are ______________ pandas than in China.

4 This year there is ______________ grass for the animals than last year.

3 Complete each sentence with *the least* or *the fewest*.

1 Of all the cows, the black one gives ___________________ milk.

2 Of all the creatures in the zoo, the snakes have ___________________ visitors.

3 Of all the puppies, this tiny one makes ___________________ noise.

4 Of all the animals in the world, pandas have ___________________ babies.

4 **Look at the picture.**

5 **Find the mistakes in these sentences.**

Four children are having a picnic.
Matt has fewer sandwiches than Lulu.
Izzy has fewer cakes than Matt.
Lulu has less fruit than Matt. Matt has less orange juice than Izzy.
Lulu has the fewest sandwiches. Matt has the fewest cakes.
Lulu has the least fruit. Izzy has the least orange juice.

6 **Write the sentences correctly.**
Use *fewer*, *less*, *the fewest* and *the least*.

____

____

____

____

____

____

____

____

____

Spelling

1 Find the 'silent *b*' words in the wordsearch. Circle them.

1 

2 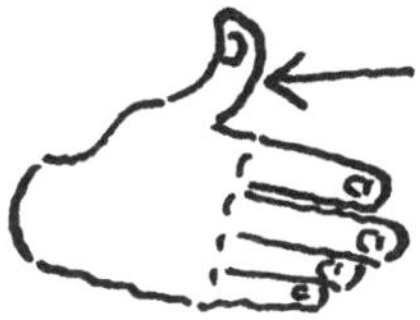

3 

4 

5 

c	r	u	m	b	t
l	a	m	b	s	z
i	f	y	z	a	o
m	w	c	o	m	b
b	l	n	r	u	d
x	t	h	u	m	b

2 Solve the clues with 'silent *b*' words.

1 We use this on our hair. _ _ _ _

2 a baby sheep _ _ _ _

3 to go up _ _ _ _ _

4 a tiny piece of cake _ _ _ _ _

5 You have got one of these on each hand. _ _ _ _ _

Writing

1 **Label the picture of the African elephant.**

tusks	small eyes	round feet	grey skin
large ears	long trunk	thin tail	

2 Write about the African elephant for an animal encyclopedia.

Facts about the African elephant

- Elephants use their trunks to get food.
- They live in herds.
- They live for 60–70 years.
- They grow to 3–4 metres high at the shoulder.
- They weigh 5–7.5 tonnes.

Unit 9

Comprehension

1 **Read Language Book 4, pages 74–75 again.**

2 **Choose the correct answer.**

1 The lion is sitting __a__

a near the Baobab tree   b under the Baobab tree

2 The rest of the pride is lying ______

a on the plain   b in the shade

3 The lions ______

a have just eaten   b are waiting to eat

4 The lions will wake up feeling ______

a tired   b refreshed

3 **Read Language Book 4, pages 74–75 again.**

4 **Tick ✔ the statements that are true.**
Put a cross ✗ if they are false.

1 The Veggy lion eats meat. __✗__
2 He never sinks his claws into another animal. ______
3 He used to be ferocious. ______
4 He likes the sight of blood. ______
5 He never attacked an elephant. ______
6 He was in the jungle hospital. ______

Vocabulary

1 Match the group with the correct collective noun.

1 cards ___d___ — a herd
2 birds ______ — b box
3 elephants ______ — c flock
4 grapes ______ — d pack
5 chocolates ______ — e bunch

2 Write the missing words.

1 a bunch of ___flowers___

2 a herd of ____________

3 a pride of ____________

4 a bag of ____________

Language building

Remember! A **statement** tells us something.
A sentence begins with a **capital letter**.
A sentence ends with a **full stop**.

A **question** asks us something.
A question begins with a **capital letter**.
A question ends with a **question mark**.

1 Look at the picture.

2 Write two sentences about the picture.

____

____

3 Write two questions about the picture.

____

____

Grammar

1 Put the words in order to make questions. Then find the correct answer to each question. Write the letter in the box.

1 see you Where the can wild elephants in ? ☐

____

2 an much weigh does How elephant ? ☐

____

3 elephant's How an trunk strong is ? ☐

____

4 live How elephants long do ? ☐

____

A They can live for up to 70 years.

B They live in Africa and India.

C An elephant can kill a lion with its trunk.

D An elephant weighs about 7,000 kg.

2 Write the questions for these answers. Use the words in the box.

What	Where
When	Which
How many	

1 _______________
I saw an elephant at the zoo.

2 _______________
There were six elephants.

3 _______________
I went to the zoo last summer.

4 _______________
They eat leaves from trees and bushes.

5 _______________
An African elephant has bigger ears.

3 Look and read.

Jim was on holiday at the seaside. He was staying with his aunt and uncle. One morning, they went down to the beach for a swim. They were walking towards the sea when Jim saw something on the sand. It was shining in the sun. He picked it up. It was a beautiful necklace! "We must take that to the police station," said his uncle. After their swim, that is what they did.

4 At the police station, a police officer asked Jim lots of questions. Read Jim's answers, and write the police officer's questions.

1 ______________________ I found it on the beach.

2 ______________________ Because we wanted to have a swim.

3 ______________________ There were a few people there.

4 ______________________ They were men.

5 ______________________ They were running along the beach.

6 ______________________ No, I didn't see their faces.

7 ______________________ I'm staying with my aunt and uncle.

8 ______________________ They live at 24 Magnolia Avenue.

9 ______________________ Their telephone number is 47 65 32.

Spelling

Small parts of words are called **syllables**.
Each syllable has a **vowel sound**.

1 Write the words. They all have one syllable.

1  fire

2  ______

3  ______

2 Write the words. They all have two syllables.

1  kettle

2  ______

3  ______

3 Write each word under the correct heading.

Read the words slowly.

~~point~~ ~~gazelle~~ told father
slow strongest penguin fruit

One-syllable words	Two-syllable words
point	gazelle
______	______
______	______
______	______

Writing

1 Write each word in the correct box.

seen	bee	shoe	spoon	fright	shed
me	true	balloon	been	night	June
few	free	bed	said	clean	light

Words that rhyme with *green*

____

____

____

Words that rhyme with *tree*

____

____

____

Words that rhyme with *red*

____

____

____

Words that rhyme with *blue*

____

____

____

Words that rhyme with *white*

____

____

____

Words that rhyme with *moon*

____

____

____

2 Write poems like this one.

Through my window I can see
Two birds sitting in a tree.

Use the rhyming words in the boxes, or think of rhyming words of your own.

1 

2 

3 

4 

Check-up 2

1 Complete the sentences using the words in the box.

bring go wear play take

1 Look at the rain!  You should take an umbrella.

2 The sun is very hot. 

You ______________________________

3 Max is very tired. 

He ______________________________

4 What's that? 

You ____________ not ____________ to school!

5 Look at those boys! 

They ____________ not ____________ in the classroom.

2 Complete each sentence with *will* and a verb from the box.

have spend rain go want shine swim be

1 The weather ______________________ fine next week.
2 It ____________ not ____________ .
3 The sun ______________________ every day.
4 The children ____________ not ____________ to school.
5 They ______________________ every day on the beach.
6 They ______________________ in the sea.
7 They ______________________ picnics on the sand.
8 They ____________ not ____________ to go home.

3 **Complete each sentence using a word from the box.**

something anything nothing somebody anybody nobody

1 I can hear footsteps! There's ____________________ upstairs.
2 Is there ____________________ in this suitcase?
3 John's school bag was empty. There was ____________________ inside.
4 Can ____________________ help Ann with her homework?
5 There's ____________________ in your pocket. What is it?
6 We heard voices but there was ____________________ in the room.

4 **Complete each sentence with *little* or *few*.**

1 We had very ____________________ time to get to the airport.
2 There were ____________________ people on the plane.
3 ____________________ animals live in the desert.
4 ____________________ rain falls there.

5 **Complete each sentence with *fewer*, *the fewest*, *less* or *the least*.**

1 There is ____________________ ice in the Arctic than there was ten years ago.
2 Because of this there are ____________________ polar bears.
3 Of all the deserts in the world the Atacama Desert has ____________________ rain.
4 It also has ____________________ visitors.

Unit 10

Comprehension

1 Read Language Book 4, pages 84–85 again.

2 Who said it?
Write the answers.

1 This is interesting. *the secretary*

2 Every day is just the same. ____________

3 I've got some news for you. ____________

4 What a nice letter! ____________

5 We'll help. ____________

6 It's an invitation to Summerfield School's Open Day. ____________

7 What soup can we make? ____________

8 Return the reply slip on the invitation, please. ____________

9 Our guest will be a professor. ____________

10 We will make vegetable soup. ____________

Vocabulary

1 Complete the crossword. Use the words in the box.

character	secretary	narrator	prop	
parents	speech	soup	penguin	scenery
guest	vegetables	setting	professor	

Clues across →

2 The person who tells the story
5 Things we eat, such as potatoes and carrots
6 A meal that you drink
7 An object that is used in a play or film
8 The person in an office who does jobs such as arranging meetings, making phone calls and preparing letters
9 A person that you invite
10 The furniture and painted background on a theatre stage
11 Mother and father

Clues down ↓

1 A person who teaches in a university
3 The time or place in which the events of a play or story happen
4 A person in a play or story
8 The words someone speaks

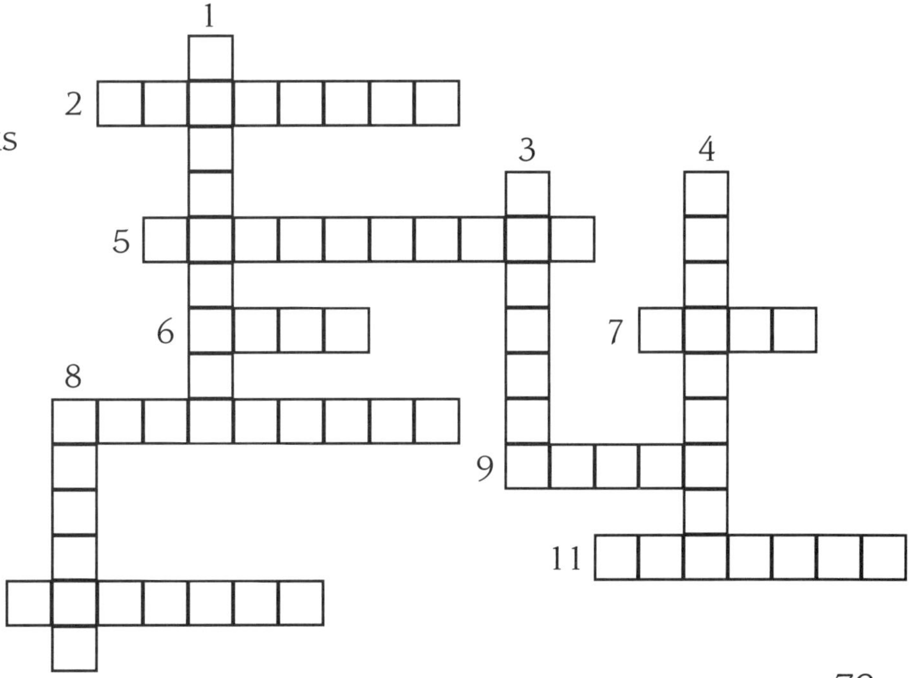

Language building

There are no rules to help us understand how to change some **singular** nouns into the **plural**.

one child (singular)

two child**ren** (plural)

1 Fill in the missing letters.

1 one child – two ch _ _ _ _ _ _

2 one man – two m _ n

3 one woman – two wom _ n

4 one tooth – two t _ _ t h

5 one foot – two f _ _ t

6 one mouse – two m _ _ _

7 one sheep – two sh _ _ p

2 Complete each sentence with the correct plural noun.

1 I have got two ________ . (foot)

2 The dentist looked at my ________ . (tooth)

3 Three ________ were shopping. (woman)

4 There are thirty ________ in my class. (child)

5 Two ________ went in the house. (man)

6 Some ________ are brown. (mouse)

7 Most ________ are white. (sheep)

Grammar

1 Match the beginning of each sentence with the correct ending.

1 If you take an umbrella, d a if the weather is fine.
2 If you don't like planes, ____ b if you ask her nicely.
3 If he has enough money, ____ c if there's a good film.
4 We'll go to the beach ____ d you won't get wet.
5 They'll go to the cinema ____ e we'll travel by train.
6 She'll help you ____ f he'll buy a guitar.

2 Put each verb into the correct tense.

1 (be, go)
If the weather __________ good, we __________ to the park.

2 (start, stay)
If it __________ to rain, we __________ at home.

3 (watch, finish)
I __________ TV if I __________ my homework.

4 (help, ask)
I __________ Mum if she __________ me.

5 (go, take)
If I __________ to Jane's party, I __________ a present.

6 (pass, study)
Billy __________ his exams if he __________ hard.

3 **Look and read. What will happen if Charlie gets up late?**

4 **Begin at the star. Write sentences.**

If he gets up late, he will ____________________

____

____

____

____

____

____

5 **What is your advice to Charlie?**

____

Spelling

1 Find the *re* words. Then write.

1	qwe(refill)rty	refill	2	uoreturnplkj	________
3	hgfdsreplyaz	________	4	xredovcbnmkj	________
5	jklreplayzxc	________	6	wrtpkhrepeat	________
7	replacemnbvc	________	8	cxzremovedrw	________
9	kremaincrwqg	________	10	mrwqxtfrepay	________

2 Complete the crossword using the *re* words above.

Clues across →

2 to come back
4 to stay
7 to pay back
10 to say again

Clues down ↓

1 to take away
3 to play again
5 to put back
6 to do again
8 to fill again
9 to answer

Writing

- The professor arrives at the school.
- The teacher welcomes the professor.
- The professor makes a short speech.
- The children serve the soup.
- Everyone enjoys the soup. It is delicious!
- The teacher and children say goodbye to the professor.

1 Read the questions.
Write the answers in the box.

1 Where does the scene take place? (the setting)

2 Who appears in the scene? (the characters)

Setting	______________________
Characters	______________________
Scenery	Classroom furniture (tables, chairs)
Props	Soup bowls and spoons

2 Think about the first thing that happens in Scene 4. Finish the stage directions below.

The teacher and the children are waiting in the classroom.

What does the teacher say to the professor when he arrives?

Teacher:

What does the professor say in his speech?

Professor:

What stage directions will you need when the children serve the soup?

What will everyone say about the soup?
What will happen at the end of the scene?
Finish the scene in your copy book.

Unit 11

Comprehension

1 Read Language Book 4, pages 92–93 again.

2 Write the correct word in each space.

1 Amy was born in ________________ (1903, 1930).

2–3 One day she saw a ________________ (TV programme, film) about a pilot who did ________________ (tricks, trucks) in an aeroplane.

4 Amy decided to be a ________________ (police officer, pilot).

5 She worked very hard and passed her ________________ (test, table).

6 Amy was an ________________ (elephant, engineer) for two years.

7 She learned how to ________________ (break, mend) engines.

8 Amy wanted to fly from ________________ (England, France) to Australia on her own.

9 She bought a plane and called it ________________ (Jason, James).

10 She planned the ________________ (aeroplane, journey) and bought the equipment.

11 Amy took off on 5 May ________________ (1903, 1930).

Vocabulary

A **compound word** is made by joining two words together.
air + field = **airfield**

1 Join the words. Write the compound words.

1 hair + brush = hairbrush
2 hand + bag = ____________
3 sea + side = ____________
4 bed + room = ____________
5 book + case = ____________
6 lady + bird = ____________
7 water + fall = ____________
8 news + paper = ____________
9 star + fish = ____________
10 moon + light = ____________
11 car + pet = ____________
12 air + port = ____________

2 Write the correct compound word under each picture.

1 ____________

2 ____________

3 ____________

4 ____________

5 ____________

6 ____________

7 ____________

8 ____________

9 ____________

10 ____________

11 ____________

12 ____________

Language building

always	tomorrow	soon	again	never
later	next	now	sometimes	today

1 Write each adverb of time in the correct space.

1 Adverb with three letters: _ _ _

2 Adverbs with four letters: _ _ _ _   _ _ _ _

3 Adverbs with five letters: _ _ _ _ _   _ _ _ _ _
_ _ _ _ _   _ _ _ _ _

4 Adverb with six letters: _ _ _ _ _ _

5 Adverb with eight letters: _ _ _ _ _ _ _ _

6 Adverb with nine letters: _ _ _ _ _ _ _ _ _

2 Complete each sentence with the correct adverb.

1 Tom __________ (next, always) goes to bed at nine o'clock.

2 It will be Wednesday __________ (tomorrow, later).

3 It will __________ (soon, now) be time to go home.

4 Mum came back into the room __________ (sometimes, later).

5 We have a holiday __________ (never, today).

Grammar

1 Circle the correct ending for each sentence.

1 Planes are faster than trains, isn't it? aren't they? aren't we?
2 The ship is sailing round the island, isn't he? isn't she? isn't it?
3 We're fond of travelling, isn't it? aren't we? aren't they?
4 Mr Jones is a good driver, isn't he? aren't they? isn't it?
5 I'm going to miss the bus, aren't we? isn't she? aren't I?

2 Add the correct ending to each sentence.

1 It's exciting to travel by ship, isn't it? ____________
2 Helicopters are slower than planes, ____________
3 Uncle Bob is learning to fly, ____________
4 We're going to drive into town, ____________
5 Grandma is going to take a taxi, ____________

3 Make sentences.

1 (car, fast)  The car is fast, isn't it?

2 (clowns, funny)  ____________

3 (kitten, soft)  ____________

4 (boy, happy)  ____________

5 (We, late)  ____________

6 (nurse, kind)  ____________

4 Look at the pictures.

Let's go for a drive!

This is my new car!

It's very fast, isn't it?

They're very wide, aren't they?

It's fantastic, isn't it?

Get in, Danny!

5 Answer the questions. Then find the right speech bubbles.

1 Did Uncle John have a new house or a new car?

2 Did Danny think it was beautiful or ugly? What did he say?

3 What did he look at first? What did he say?

4 Did he look inside the car? What did he say?

5 What did Uncle John say when he held up the keys?

6 Did Uncle John get into the big black car or the little white car? What did he say?

6 Write the story.

Spelling

1 Make some words.

1 r, f, pl, tr → ace → race, ______, ______, ______

2 n, m, r, pr → ice → ______, ______, ______, ______

2 Now choose one of the words to complete each sentence.

1 ______ have four legs and long tails.
2 My nose is in the middle of my ______ .
3 I ran fast in the ______ .
4 I like chicken and ______ .
5 Cairo is a good ______ to live.
6 I think the cake tastes ______ .
7 I can ______ the picture with my pencil.
8 I looked at the ______ of the toy – it was too expensive!

3 Now write the words in alphabetical order.

1 ______ 2 ______ 3 ______ 4 ______
5 ______ 6 ______ 7 ______ 8 ______

Writing

1 **Read these notes. Complete the sentences about Mother Teresa as a child.**

- Born in 1910
- Lived in Serbia
- Real name – Agnes Bojaxhiu
- Always helped parents at home
- Always wanted to help other people

1 Mother Teresa was born in ______________ .

2 She lived in ______________ .

3 Her real name was ______________ ______________ .

4 Agnes always helped her ______________ at ______________ .

5 She always ______________ to help ______________ ______________ , too.

2 **Read these notes and write a paragraph about Mother Teresa's work in India.**

- Went to live in Calcutta, India
- Helped poor people
- Built her own hospital for the poor
- People called her Mother Teresa
- Calcutta – full of poor people
- Worked in hospitals and schools
- Was like a mother to the people

3 **Read these notes and write a paragraph about Mother Teresa's achievements.**

- All her life – helped other people
- 1979 – received special prize for her good work
- Gave all her money to poor people
- Was very famous
- Died in 1997

Unit 12

Comprehension

1 Read Language Book 4, pages 100–101 again.

2 Put the sentences in order.

___ Aunt Em climbed down the ladder into the cellar.
___ Dorothy caught Toto and picked him up.
___ Then they heard the wind whistling from the south.
___ Aunt Em came to the door.
_1_ Uncle Henry and Dorothy heard the wind coming from the north.
___ Aunt Em saw the cyclone coming closer.
___ Dorothy fell over and sat on the floor.
___ Toto the dog hid under the bed.
___ The wind shook the house hard.
___ Uncle Henry ran towards the sheds.

Vocabulary

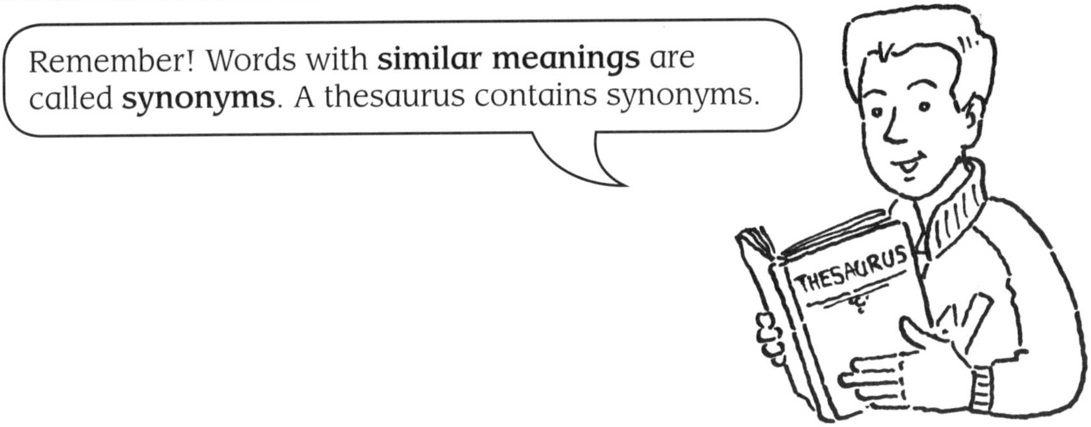

1 Match the pairs of words with similar meanings. Write the letters.

1 afraid	g	a cyclone
2 powerful	___	b shed
3 tornado	___	c strong
4 hut	___	d centre
5 raise	___	e gentle
6 middle	___	f scream
7 tender	___	g scared
8 yell	___	h lift

2 Replace each underlined word with a word that has a similar meaning. Use the words above.

1 'There's a <u>cyclone</u> tornado coming, Em,' Uncle Henry shouted.
2 A hurricane is a very <u>strong</u> ________ wind.
3 Dorothy stood in the <u>centre</u> ________ of the room.
4 Dorothy was a very <u>gentle</u> ________ girl.
5 I will <u>yell</u> ________ if I see a mouse.
6 Aunt Em was <u>afraid</u> ________ of the cyclone.
7 'I cannot <u>raise</u> ________ this heavy rock,' Dorothy said.
8 Uncle Henry kept some chickens in the <u>shed</u> ________ .

Language building

Remember! Sometimes we split **direct speech** into **two parts**.
'**Quick, Dorothy**,' Aunt Em said, '**go to the cellar**!'

1 The direct speech in each of these sentences is in two parts. Put the direct speech back together.

1 'Come here,' said Dorothy, 'and look at the garden.'

Dorothy said, 'Come here and look at the garden.'

2 'I think,' Aunt Em said, 'the wind has stopped.'

____

3 'I will go to the shed,' said Uncle Henry, 'and milk the cows.'

____

4 'I don't like milk,' said Dorothy, 'but I do like tea.'

____

5 'If it rains tomorrow,' Aunt Em said, 'I will stay indoors.'

____

6 'Get up, Dorothy,' Uncle Henry said, 'and get dressed.'

____

7 'When I fell off my bike,' said Dorothy, 'I got muddy.'

____

8 'It's a lovely day today,' said Aunt Em, 'isn't it?'

____

Grammar

1 Add *too* or *enough* to the sentences.

1  Don't go swimming. It's dangerous.

Don't go swimming. It's too dangerous.

2  He can't go to school. He is ill.

____

3  It can't speak. It isn't intelligent.

____

4  You can't go outside. The hurricane is powerful.

____

5  This horse won't win the race. It's not fast.

____

6  Can I have some sugar? The strawberries aren't sweet.

____

2 Complete each sentence with *too* or *enough* and a word from the box.

loud	expensive	rough
juicy	difficult	old

1 You can't go sailing. The waves are ______________________________

2 I can't hear the music. It isn't ______________________________

3 They can't travel alone. They aren't ______________________________

4 He couldn't buy the car because it was ______________________________

5 She couldn't do her homework because it was ______________________________

6 I didn't like the oranges. They weren't ______________________________

3 Look at the pictures and read the speech bubbles.

4 Answer the questions.

1 Where did Sally and her mother go? Why?

2 Did she try on lots of shoes or only a few? Was the first pair too big or too small?

3 Was the second pair too big or too small?

4 What was wrong with the third pair?

5 Was the fourth pair comfortable enough?

6 What was the last pair of shoes like?

5 Write the story. Give it a title. ______________________________

Spelling

1 Complete each word with a silent *l* or *t*. Read the words aloud.

1 ca l m 2 of __ en 3 pa __ m 4 wres __ le
5 ha __ f 6 ta __ k 7 cas __ le 8 wa __ k
9 lis __ en 10 whis __ le

2 Now write the correct word under each picture.

 1 ____________	 2 ____________	 3 ____________
 4 ____________	 5 ____________	 6 ____________
 7 ____________	 8 ____________	 9 ____________

Write the word you didn't use.

____

Writing

1 The cyclone picked up the house and took it a long way away. Imagine this is what Dorothy saw when she opened the door. Label the picture. Use the words in the box.

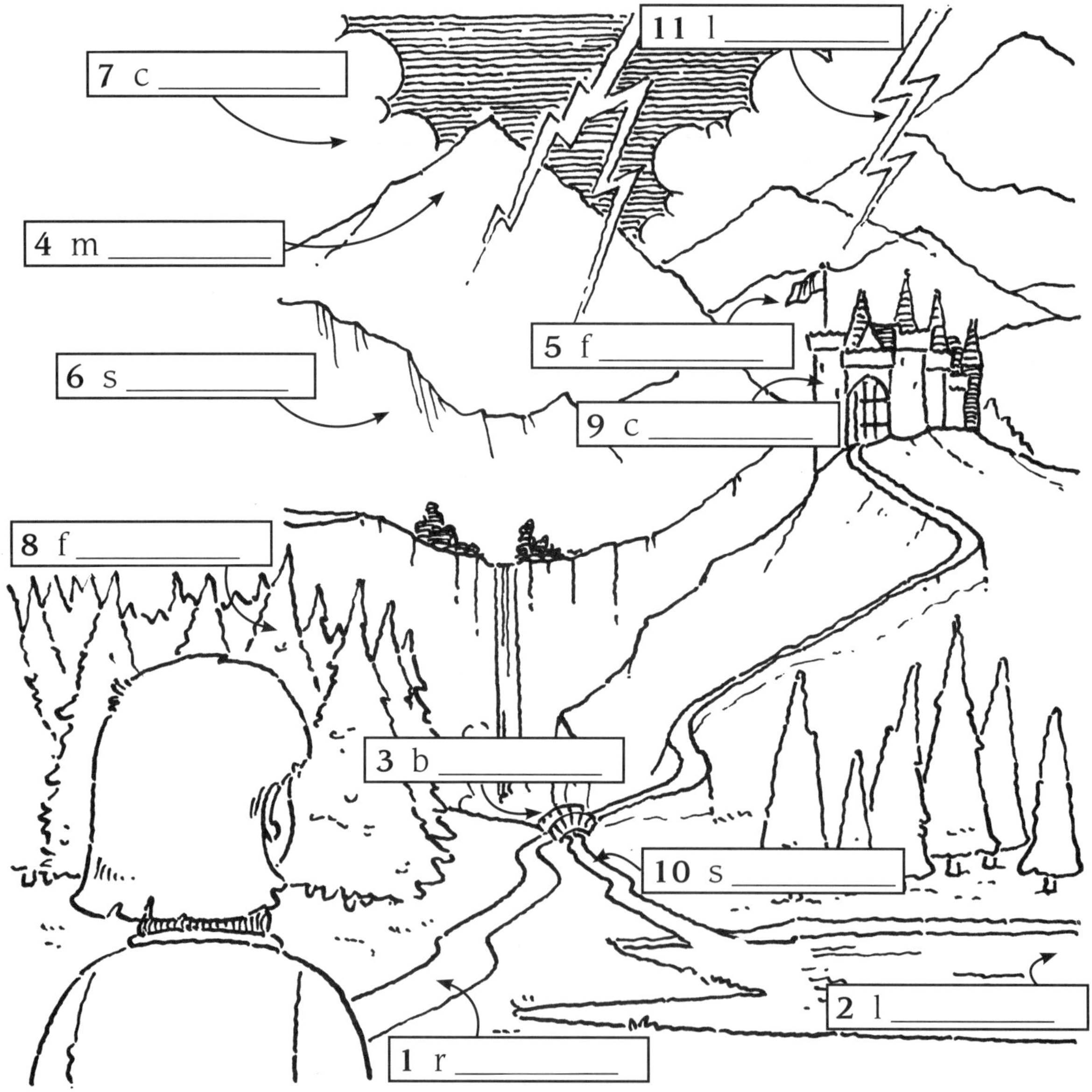

mountains	snow	lake	clouds	flag	castle
stream	lightning	forest	bridge	road	

2 Describe what Dorothy saw.

dark strange black tall high wooden

When Dorothy opened the door, this is what she saw.

Unit 13

Comprehension

1 **Read Language Book 4, pages 108–109 again.**

2 **Match the beginning of each sentence with the correct ending.**

1	The storm arrived at 4 o'clock	c	a	hit his house.
2	The hurricane damaged houses	___	b	many cars.
3	Mr Brown was asleep when the hurricane	___	c	yesterday morning.
4	The wind blew the roof off	___	d	all over the island.
5	The Brown family went to the school	___	e	onto the beach.
6	The strong wind made huge waves	___	f	Mr Brown's house.
7	The wind blew some boats	___	g	to sleep.
8	Trees fell down and smashed	___	h	Mr King's lorry.
9	The hurricane blew a tree onto	___	i	in the sea.
10	Many people were injured and went	___	j	to the hospital.

Vocabulary

Sometimes we can **group words together**.

teacher school student

1 Underline the odd one out.

1	roof	window	tree	door
2	storm	sunshine	hurricane	cyclone
3	car	lorry	bus	boat
4	knife	tea	coffee	water
5	mango	potato	banana	apple
6	hat	head	foot	hand
7	night	morning	afternoon	rain
8	football	tennis	swimming	cellar
9	eye	nose	dog	ear
10	bowl	spoon	cup	plate
11	January	spring	summer	winter
12	potato	road	carrot	cabbage
13	uncle	brother	king	grandfather
14	shoes	boots	slippers	shirt
15	hen	duck	turkey	cow

Language building

Remember! We can write speech in two ways.
Direct speech
Mike said, 'A tree fell on my lorry.'
Reported speech
Mike said that a tree fell on his lorry.

1 **Write *D* if the sentence contains direct speech.
Write *R* if it contains reported speech.**

1 Mr Brown said, 'I was sleeping in bed and I heard a loud noise.' D

2 Mr Brown said that his family went to the school to sleep. ___

3 Mrs Downing said that her husband tried to save his boat. ___

4 'My husband is a sailor,' Mrs Downing said. ___

5 'Have you ever seen such devastation?' Mrs Downing asked. ___

2 **Match the sentences containing direct speech with the sentences containing reported speech.**

1 Paul said, 'I watched a good film last night.' c

2 James said, 'I can run fast.' ___

3 'I'm eighty years old,' the old lady said. ___

4 'I won the swimming race,' Anna said. ___

a James said that he can run fast.
b The old lady said that she is eighty years old.
c Paul said that he watched a good film last night.
d Anna said that she won the swimming race.

Grammar

1 Complete each sentence using a verb from the box.

smashed	arrived	opened	climbed
jumped	crashed	washed	

1  Look! The sea has smashed the boat.

2  Look! The car has ________________ into the tree.

3  Grandma and Grandpa have ________________ .

4  The dog has ________________ into the pond.

5  Look! We have ________________ our hands.

6 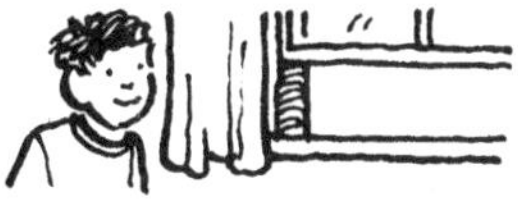 I have ________________ the window.

7  They have ________________ the mountain.

2 Complete each sentence using a verb from the box.

eaten	been	broken
drunk	seen	gone

1 Have you ever ________________ a shark?
2 Have you ever ________________ in a hurricane?
3 Jim has never ________________ a pineapple.
4 I have never ________________ coconut milk.
5 Sally is not here. She has ________________ to school.
6 Look! The boys have ________________ a window.

3 **Look at the pictures.**

4 **Answer the questions.**

1 Is the weather stormy or calm? Where has a tree fallen?

2 Is the sea rough or calm? Where have the waves thrown this boat?

3 Is it raining lightly or heavily? What has this house lost?

4 What has the wind broken? What is the man sweeping up?

5 **Write about the pictures.**

In the first picture ______________________________

____

In the second picture ______________________________

____

In the third picture ______________________________

____

In the fourth picture ______________________________

____

Spelling

1 **Complete each word with *or*. Read aloud the words you make.**

1 sail_or_ 2 edit___ 3 act___ 4 visit___ 5 doct___
6 auth___ 7 tail___ 8 may___ 9 invent___

2 **Now write the words in the correct spaces.**

1 Words with five letters: _ _ _ _ _ _ _ _ _ _
2 Words with six letters: _ _ _ _ _ _ _ _ _ _ _ _
_ _ _ _ _ _ _ _ _ _ _ _
_ _ _ _ _ _
3 Word with seven letters: _ _ _ _ _ _ _
4 Word with eight letters: _ _ _ _ _ _ _ _

3 **Complete each sentence with the correct word.**

1 A ______________ sails on a ship.
2 An ______________ writes books.
3 An ______________ invents things.
4 A ______________ makes people better.
5 A ______________ makes clothes.
6 An ______________ acts.
7 A ______________ is someone who comes to visit you.
8 An ______________ helps to get a book or magazine ready to print.
9 A ______________ is an important person in some towns.

Writing

1 **Complete this newspaper report with words from the box.**

cat	wheel	police	glass	car	driver
crash	face	road	baby	hospital	window

CAR CRASHES INTO CAKE SHOP

Yesterday afternoon there was a bad car **(1)** ______________ in the High Street. A black **(2)** ______________ ran across the road. A **(3)** ______________ went off the road and crashed into the **(4)** ______________ of a cake shop. The **(5)** ______________ of the car, Mr Banks, said that he was driving along the High Street when a cat ran across the **(6)** ______________ in front of his car. 'I turned my steering **(7)** ______________ and tried to miss the cat. Then I crashed into the shop window,' Mr Banks said.

Mrs Hills saw the accident. She was walking past the cake shop with her **(8)** ______________ . 'I saw the car. It was coming towards me. I grabbed my baby and ran. It was lucky we were not hurt,' she said.

The owner of the cake shop, Mrs Bun, is in **(9)** ______________ . When the car crashed into the window of her shop, some **(10)** ______________ cut her face. 'I heard a crash and saw the car. It was coming through my window!' Mrs Bun said. 'My **(11)** ______________ is badly cut.'

The High Street was closed for two hours after the accident.

The **(12)** ______________ have now moved the car and cleared all the broken glass.

2 Write your own newspaper report about the car accident.

Write a title. →

Draw a picture. Show the car crashing into the shop window. →

Write an interesting first paragraph. →

Write a paragraph about what Mrs Banks saw. She was in the car with her husband. →

Check-up 3

1 Put each verb into the correct tense.

1 (go, learn)

If they ___go___ to France, they ___will learn___ to speak French.

2 (travel, take)

If John ________ by car, the journey ________ eight hours.

3 (get, fly)

He ________ there more quickly if he ________ .

4 (work, pass)

If Jenny ________ not ________ , she ________ not ________ her exams.

5 (buy, be)

I ________ not ________ the shoes if they ________ too small.

6 (feel, stay)

You ________ tired tomorrow if you ________ up late tonight.

2 Add the correct ending to each sentence.

1 The bike is very old, ___isn't it?___

2 We're going to buy a new car, ________________

3 You're feeling ill, ________________

4 It's a beautiful day, ________________

5 Lisa is a good singer, ________________

6 The lions are sleeping, ________________

7 Dad is reading the newspaper, ________________

3 Add *too* or *enough* to the second sentence in each pair.

1  He can't lift the box. It is heavy.

He can't lift the box. It is too heavy.

2  She can't reach the book. She isn't tall.

____

3  He doesn't go to school yet. He is young.

____

4  I can't wear this jumper. It is small.

____

5  We can't go to the beach. The weather isn't warm.

____

6  The car won't move. It is old.

____

4 Complete each sentence with a word from each box.

have has + eaten picked broken locked brushed gone

1  Look! Someone has broken the window.

2  Who ____________________ all the cakes?

3 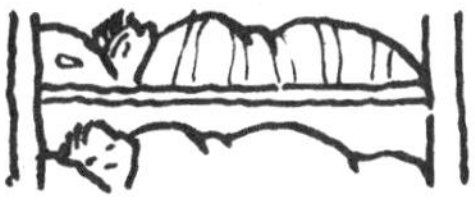 The boys ____________________ to bed.

4  Mr Harris ____________________ the door.

5  Look! We ____________________ our teeth.

6  The girls ____________________ some apples.

Unit 14

Comprehension

1 **Read Language Book 4, pages 118–119 again.**

2 **Match the sentences to the people.**

a He has a twin sister.
b His friend is called Vialli.
c She went to the football match with her husband.
d She was hit on the head with a football.
e He is Italian.
f He reads the newspaper.
g She shouted, 'Look out!'
h He plays football for his school team.
i He is a footballer and his family live in Denstone.
j She asked her Dad to take her to a football match.
k He gave Stacey the match ball.
l He sat next to Stacey at the hospital.

Mum	Dad	Steve	Stacey	Brent	Vialli
___ ___	___ ___	a ___	___ ___	___ ___	___ ___

Vocabulary

Remember!
Some words **sound the same** but are **spelled differently** and have different meanings.

1 Match the words that sound the same.

1 to	c	a	their
2 here	___	b	through
3 they're	___	c	too
4 blew	___	d	your
5 threw	___	e	hear
6 you're	___	f	blue

2 Choose the correct word.

1 Vialli spoke ___to___ (to, too) Brent.
2 'Come ______________ (hear, here)!' Stacey shouted.
3 They love football. ______________ (Their, They're) football fans.
4 The sky is ______________ (blew, blue).
5 Steve ______________ (threw, through) the ball to Stacey.
6 'I think ______________ (your, you're) funny,' Vialli said to Stacey.
7 Stacey and Steve went to the match with ______________ (they're, their) Dad.
8 The two footballers came ______________ (threw, through) the door.
9 'Look out!' Mum shouted – but it was ______________ (to, too) late.
10 'What's ______________ (you're, your) name?' Steve asked.
11 I can ______________ (here, hear) a noise.
12 The referee ______________ (blew, blue) his whistle.

Language building

An **adverb of place** tells us **where** something happened. For example, Mum sat **here**.

inside	everywhere	away	forwards
~~outside~~	upwards	right	nearby
there	here	where	backwards

1 Choose the most suitable adverb of place.

1 We went ___outside___ to play.

2 'Come ______________ and look at this big spider!' Sam shouted.

3 I looked ______________ but I did not see Jack.

4 I want to go to France. I want to go ______________ next year.

5 I can't remember ______________ I put my book.

6 I slipped and fell ______________ .

7 The car turned ______________ .

8 The lorry began to move ______________ .

9 When it began to rain we went ______________ .

10 Mr Smith said that he lived ______________ .

11 No one came to the door so Sam walked ______________ .

12 The men began to climb ______________ .

Grammar

1 Complete each question with a verb from the box.

1 Have you ______________ with the newspaper yet?

2 Has the match ______________ yet?

3 Haven't you ______________ your teeth yet?

4 Have the children ______________ to school yet?

5 Has Sally ______________ that email yet?

gone
sent
started
finished
brushed

2 Complete each sentence with a verb from the box.

1 I haven't ______________ this book yet.

2 Billy hasn't ______________ his homework yet.

3 We haven't ______________ to your teacher yet.

4 Jenny hasn't ______________ home from school yet.

5 Grandma and Grandpa haven't ______________ yet.

spoken
arrived
read
come
done

3 What have they just done? Complete each sentence using a verb from the box.

made	scored	found	caught	broken

1  He has just broken a plate.

2  He ______________________________

3  They ______________________________

4  She ______________________________

5  I ______________________________

4 Look and read.

Arnie and Baz are scuba divers. They had an interesting dive recently. They wanted to find a ship. The ship sank hundreds of years ago with – or so people say – a chest full of gold coins and jewels. Arnie and Baz wanted to find this treasure. Arnie took an underwater camera and filmed their dive.

5 Look at these pictures from Arnie's film. Answer the questions.

1 Has Baz found the ship yet?
What has he just come face to face with?

____

____

2 What has Baz just seen?
Is he swimming away from the ship or towards it?

____

____

3 Is Baz inside or outside the wreck?
Has he found the treasure chest yet?

____

____

4 What has Baz just spotted?
Has he opened it yet?

____

____

5 What has Baz just done?
What has he just found?

____

____

Spelling

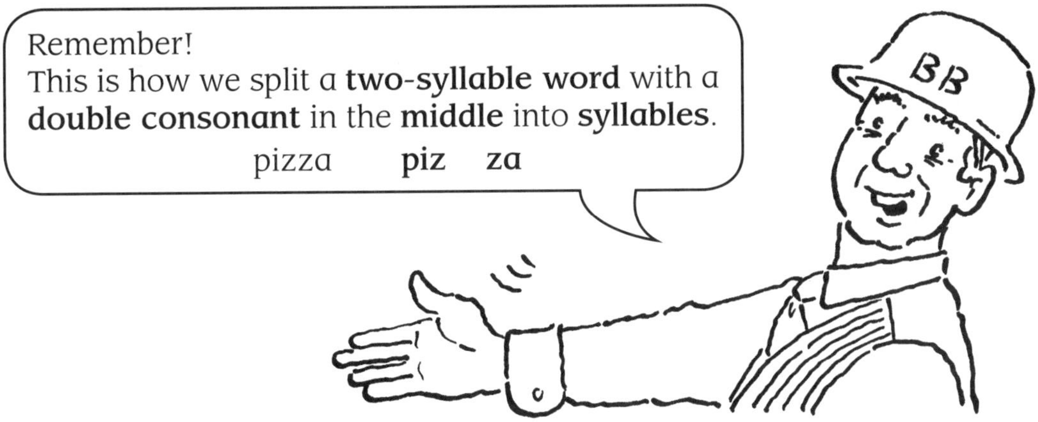

1 Split these words into two syllables.

1 tunnel = tun + nel
2 apple = ________ + ________
3 pizza = ________ + ________
4 rabbit = ________ + ________
5 yellow = ________ + ________
6 butter = ________ + ________
7 coffee = ________ + ________
8 mirror = ________ + ________

2 Write the words that contain these double consonants.

1 bb rabbit
2 ff ____________
3 ll ____________
4 nn ____________
5 pp ____________
6 rr ____________
7 tt ____________
8 zz ____________

3 Now write each of the words in the correct place.

1 I am a colour. yellow
2 I am a fruit. ____________
3 You drink me. ____________
4 I have got four legs and a tail. ____________
5 You put me on bread. ____________
6 A train goes through me. ____________
7 I have got cheese on top. ____________
8 You look at me and see yourself. ____________

Writing

1 **Complete this story plan for another story called 'It's a knockout'. Choose and write the correct word.**

Part 1

Steve and Stacey love __________ (swimming, tennis).

Dad tells the children that their favourite tennis player, Pete Samms, is coming to their __________ (town, road).

Steve and Stacey ask _________ (Mum, Dad) to take them to see Pete Samms.

Part 2

The ___________ (family, father) go to see the match.

Pete Samms dives and _______ (kicks, hits) the ball.

The ball hits Stacey in the _________ (foot, face).

2 **Make up your own ending for the story.**

Part 3

____

____

____

____

____

____

Use the story plan to help you write the story.
Continue the story in your copybook, if necessary.

It's a knockout

Unit 15

Comprehension

1 Read Language Book 4, pages 126–127 again.

2 Write *T* if the statement is true.
Write *F* if the statement is false.

1 One billion people watch the Olympic Games on TV. ___

2 The Olympic Games started two thousand years ago. ___

3 The Olympic Games started in Rome. ___

4 In the ancient Olympic Games, there were races for women. ___

5 Baron de Coubertin loved sport. ___

6 The Olympic Games happen every six years. ___

7 Soccer is one of the sports in the Olympic Games. ___

8 The Olympic flag has got five rings. ___

9 The rings on the Olympic flag represent five different countries. ___

10 At the end of the Olympic Games, an athlete lights the Olympic Flame. ___

Vocabulary

It is important to be able to use **alphabetical order**. The words in a **dictionary** or **thesaurus** are arranged in alphabetical order.

1 **Put these words in alphabetical order.**

boxing	tennis	swimming	wrestling	archery	volleyball

1 ____________ 2 ____________ 3 ____________

4 ____________ 5 ____________ 6 ____________

2 **Put these words in alphabetical order.**
You will need to look at the second letter of each word.

chicken	cow	crocodile	camel

1 ____________ 2 ____________ 3 ____________ 4 ____________

3 **Put these words in alphabetical order.**
You will need to look at the third letter of each word.

gorilla	goat	goose	goldfish

1 ____________ 2 ____________ 3 ____________ 4 ____________

4 **Write the days of the week in alphabetical order.**

1 ________________ 2 ________________

3 ________________ 4 ________________

5 ________________ 6 ________________

7 ________________

Language building

This is the **verb**.

The runner won a medal.

This is the **subject**.
The subject is the main person or thing in the sentence.

This is the **object**.
The object usually comes after the verb.

1 **Underline the subject, circle the verb and draw a rectangle round the object in each sentence.**

1 The athlete was holding the Olympic Flag.
2 The lady was eating an ice cream.
3 The man is driving his van.
4 Mrs Smith drank a cup of tea.
5 Sam won the race.
6 The boy lost his pencil.

2 **Choose the most suitable object from the box.**

the queen	a letter	the plane
my chair	a picture	~~his newspaper~~

1 Mr Jones read his newspaper.
2 The pilot flew ______________.
3 The king spoke to ______________.
4 I fell off ______________.
5 I painted ______________.
6 Anna wrote ______________.

Grammar

1 Complete each sentence with *What a*, *What an* or *What*.

1  __________ fast runner!

2  __________ fast runners!

3  __________ interesting sport!

4  __________ unusual clothes!

5  __________ great stadium!

6  __________ incredible jump!

2 Complete each sentence with *What a* or *What*.

1  __________ calm water!

2  __________ excitement!

3  __________ strong man!

4  __________ perfect weather!

5  __________ beautiful horse!

6 

__________ fantastic score!

3 Write sentences beginning with *What a*, *What an* or *What*.

1  ______________________________

2  ______________________________

3  ______________________________

4  ______________________________

4 Look at the pictures.

5 Answer the questions. Find the correct speech bubbles.

1 Where were Billy and Bob? Was the match boring or exciting?

2 What did the referee look at? Was the game nearly over?

3 Where did a blue player run? Did he run fast? What did Dad say?

4 Did the player miss or did he score a goal? What did Billy shout?

5 What did the referee blow? Was the game over?

6 Who were the winners, the whites or the blues? What did the boys say?

6 Write the story. Give it a title.

Spelling

In some words, the **o** sounds like a **u**.

1 **Circle each *o* that sounds like a *u*.**

nothing money month wonderful

son love tongue

2 **Look at the words above. Write the word that:**

1 ends with ***ue***. tongue

2 has got only three letters. ____________

3 contains ***one***. ____________

4 begins with ***no***. ____________

5 starts with ***l***. ____________

6 begins with ***m*** and ends with ***th***. ____________

7 ends with ***ful***. ____________

3 **Now complete each sentence with one of the words.**

1 I love chocolate!

2 Mr and Mrs Shah have two daughters and one ____________ .

3 January is the first ____________ of the year.

4 I have got a ____________ in my mouth.

5 The poor man has got no ____________ .

6 The sunset was ____________ .

7 If you take ten from ten, you are left with ____________ .

Writing

This **chart** shows the names some women who won medals in the 2004 Olympic Games in Athens.

1 Complete the chart with the details of these three medal winners.

In the 20 km walk, a Greek woman, Athanasia Tsoumeleka, won the gold medal. In second place with the silver medal was Olimpiada Ivanova of Russia. An Australian, Jane Saville, came third and won the bronze medal.

Event	Name	Country	Medal
800 m race	Kelly Holmes	Great Britain	Gold
800 m race	Hasna Benhassi	Morocco	Silver
800 m race	Joland Ceplak	Slovakia	Bronze
1500 m race	Kelly Holmes	Great Britain	Gold
1500 m race	Tatyana Tomaschova	Russia	Silver
1500 m race	Maria Cioncan	Rumania	Bronze
100 m hurdles	Joanna Hayes	USA	Gold
100 m hurdles	Olena Krasovka	Ukraine	Silver
100 m hurdles	Melissa Morrison	USA	Bronze
Discus	Natalya Sadova	Russia	Gold
Discus	Anastasia Kelesidou	Greece	Silver
Discus	Olga Yatchenko	Bellarusse	Bronze
High jump	Yelena Slesarenko	Russia	Gold
High jump	Hestrie Cloete	RSA	Silver
High jump	Viktorya Styopina	Ukraine	Bronze
20 km walk			
20 km walk			
20 km walk			

2 Write eight interesting facts you have found out from the chart.

1 In the 100m hurdles, two women from the USA won medals. Joanna Hayes came first and won a gold medal. Melissa Morrison came third and won a bronze medal.

2 ______________________________

3 ______________________________

4 ______________________________

5 ______________________________

6 ______________________________

7 ______________________________

8 ______________________________

Unit 16

Comprehension

1 **Read Language Book 4, pages 134–135 again.**

2 **Choose the correct word.**

1 The rocket landed in the middle of the ________________ (day, night).

2 The Martian had ________________ (red, green) skin.

3 The Martian was extremely ________________ (naughty, nervous).

4 The Martian went in the ________________ (back, front) door of the supermarket.

5 When the baby saw the Martian, the baby began to ________________ (cry, laugh).

6 The Martian was ________________ (thirsty, hungry).

7 A girl called ________________ (Jane, Judy) stopped right beside the Martian.

8 Judy was pushing a ________________ (trolley, pram).

9 Judy ________________ (hated, loved) shopping.

10 Judy bundled the Martian into a ________________ (bag, box).

Vocabulary

1 Find twelve 'speaking' verbs. **Write them here.**

1	qwrsaidtphlw	said
2	zxmqaskedmnb	__________
3	shoutedvbcx	__________
4	pytrwdyelled	__________
5	vcwhisperedz	__________
6	wqmurmuredpo	__________
7	kjhsgrumbled	__________
8	ytrmoanedbgq	__________
9	bnrepliedmjd	__________
10	answeredwqor	__________
11	nmbcdcriedzs	__________
12	trwsobbedqdk	__________

2 Complete each sentence with the most suitable 'speaking' verb.

1 'What's your name?' Judy ___asked___ (said, asked) the Martian.

2 'I haven't got a name,' the Martian __________ (moaned, replied).

3 'I'm very unhappy!' the Martian __________ (sobbed, yelled).

4 'I don't want to go to bed!' Judy __________ (moaned, said).

5 'Run! A monster is coming!' Judy __________ (shouted, murmured) to her friend.

Language building

Remember!
A **possessive adjective** tells us who possesses (or owns) something.

The Martian wore a jersey. **His** jersey was red.

His tells you more about the jersey.

Possessive adjectives

my your his her its our their

1 Underline the possessive adjective in each of these sentences.

1 I picked up my book and went to bed.

2 The children emptied their bags.

3 The lady lost her coat.

4 The bird laid its eggs in the nest.

5 'Is this your coat?' Mrs Shah asked Emma.

6 'Our painting is the best,' the boys said.

7 The man took off his cap.

2 Complete each sentence with the correct possessive adjective.

1 'This is ___our___ (my / our) toy,' said the twins.

2 The man said that it was __________ (his / its) coat.

3 The girl lost __________ (her / its) bike.

4 'Is this __________ (your / our) ruler?' the teacher asked Amy.

5 The teacher held up a book and said to Tom, 'Is this __________ (your / its) book?'

6 The dog wagged __________ (my / its) tail.

Grammar

1 **Make questions beginning with *Would you like*.**

1  ______________________________

2  ______________________________

3  ______________________________

4  ______________________________

2 **Make suggestions beginning with *How about* or *What about*.**

1 Let's have a picnic! How about having a picnic?

2 Let's go to the beach! ______________________________

3 Let's build a sandcastle! ______________________________

4 Let's buy an ice cream! ______________________________

5 Let's sit in the shade! ______________________________

3 **Make suggestions beginning *Shall we* or *Let's*.**

Remember!
Shall we + question mark **(?)**
Let's + exclamation mark **(!)**

1 It's a lovely day. Let's go to the park!

2 There's a good programme on TV. ______________________________

3 It's Mum's birthday next week. ______________________________

4 I feel like a game of tennis. ______________________________

5 I need some new shoes. ______________________________

4 Look at this.

5 Write their suggestions.

Let's ______________________________

How about ______________________________

Shall we ______________________________

What about ______________________________

Shall we ______________________________

Let's ______________________________

Spelling

1 Complete each word with the correct vowel. Then write the word.

o a **1** import a nt important	i e **2** vall __ y ________	a u **3** c __ ndle ________
u i **4** hosp __ tal ________	o a **5** m __ gic ________	a e **6** larg __ ________
i e **7** rac __ ________	o a **8** newsp __ per ________	e i **9** gard __ n ________
o u **10** m __ nth ________	a i **11** expens __ ve ________	o a **12** w __ lk ________

2 Now read each word aloud. Write it in the correct column.

Listen to the number of syllables in each word.

One-syllable words	Two-syllable words	Three-syllable words
________	________	important
________	________	________
________	________	________
________	________	________

Writing

Judy and her friend John land on a strange planet in their rocket. They open the hatch and get out.

1 **Read what each person says in the speech bubbles. Write what each person says below each picture.**

'What a strange place!' John exclaimed.

'____' Judy replied.

'____________________' shouted John. '____________________.'

'____' Judy said.

'____' John exclaimed.

'____' Judy added.

2 Continue the story. Write what you think John and Judy say.

The monster saw John and Judy behind the rock.

It looked at Judy and said, 'Hello! Who are you?'

'Where are you from?' it asked.

The monster scratched its head and said, 'How did you get here?'

'My name's Xang. What's your name?' it asked John.

The monster smiled.
'Would you like to come and meet my friend Xing?' it asked.

3 Write what you think happens next in your copybook.

Unit 17

Comprehension

1 **Read Language Book 4, pages 142–143 again.**

2 **Which animal does each sentence tell you about?**

chimpanzees

1 ___ ___ ___

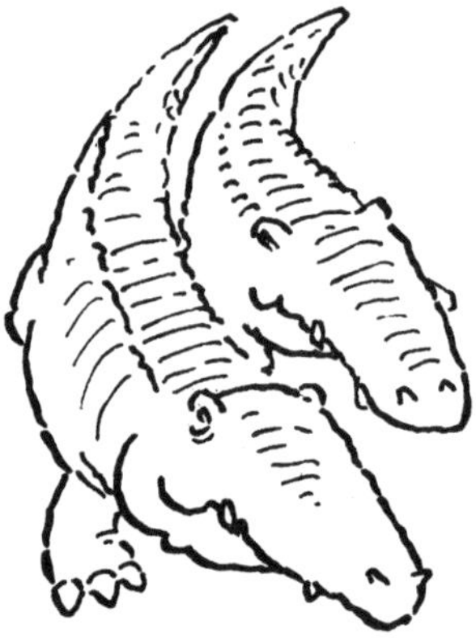

crocodiles

2 a ___ ___

tigers

3 ___ ___ ___

elephants

4 ___ ___ ___

a They live in water.
b They have got wrinkled skin.
c They have got long arms.
d They have got stripy coats.
e They have got big ears.
f They eat raw meat.
g Their skin is used to make shoes and handbags.
h They groom each other.
i They are used for medical experiments.
j They have got sharp teeth.
k Some people hunt them for their fur.
l People use their tusks to make ornaments.

Vocabulary

1 **Choose and write the correct antonym for each word. Use the thesaurus to help you.**

hot ~~bored~~ tame rough miserable blunt weak cloudy

1 excited	bored	2 sharp	______	3 cold	______
4 strong	______	5 happy	______	6 fierce	______
7 gentle	______	8 sunny	______		

2 **Replace the adjective in each sentence with a word that means the opposite.**

1 It was a very ~~hot~~ cold day.
2 The children were bored ______ .
3 My pencil was blunt ______ .
4 The weather was cloudy ______ .
5 The old man was weak ______ .
6 I like to be rough ______ when I play.
7 On my birthday I felt miserable ______ .
8 The lion was tame ______ .

Language building

Remember!
A **possessive noun** tells us who **owns** something.
If the noun is plural (there is more than one owner):

Rule 1
We add *'* to the noun if it ends with *s*.

the **monkeys'** tails
(The tails belong to the monkeys.)

Rule 2
We add *'s* to the noun if it does not end with *s*.

the **children's** hats
(The hats belong to the children.)

1 Write the sentence. Use Rule 1.

1 the girls' bikes — The bikes belong to the girls.
2 the teachers' room — ______
3 the dragons' cave — ______
4 the sailors' ship — ______
5 the birds' nest — ______
6 the boys' books — ______
7 the cats' home — ______

2 Write the phrase. Use Rule 2.

1 the sheep's wool — The wool belongs to the sheep.
2 ______ — The house belongs to the men.
3 ______ — The bags belong to the women.
4 ______ — The hay belongs to the deer.
5 ______ — The coffee machine belongs to the staff.
6 ______ — The ball belongs to the children.
7 ______ — The carts belong to the oxen.

Grammar

1 Complete each sentence with a verb from the box.

watching diving taking swinging climbing

1 We enjoyed ______________ the animals at the zoo.
2 The chimpanzees were good at ______________ trees.
3 They loved ______________ on ropes, too.
4 The penguins liked ______________ into the pool.
5 The elephants were only interested in ______________ food from their keeper.

2 Complete each sentence using a verb ending in *ing*.

1 Jenny loves ____________________

2 Phil is interested in ____________________

3 Susie likes ____________________ the piano.

4 Max enjoys ____________________ TV.

5 Henry is good at ____________________

3 What are they good at doing?

1  Lisa can read music very well and she has a lovely voice.

She is good at ____________________

2  Teddy passes the ball well and scores lots of goals.

____

3  Molly likes being in the kitchen. Her cakes are delicious.

____

4 Look at this chart. Complete the sentences.

This is Katie

likes	
enjoys	
loves	
is good at	
is interested in	

Katie likes ______________________________ . She enjoys ______________________ . She loves ______________________________ .
She is good at ______________________ . She is interested in ______________________________ .

5 Look at this chart. Write sentences.

This is Derek

likes	
enjoys	
loves	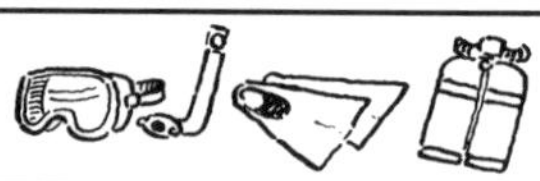
is good at	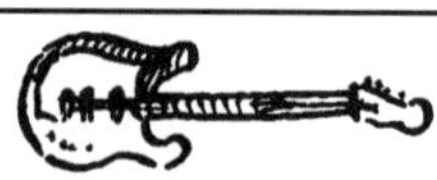
is interested in	

____

____

____

____

____

Spelling

1 Find eight *al* words.

1 qwecalwaysrt
2 uocomicalplk
3 hgfdsalmostz
4 xmusicalvcbn
5 jklalreadyzx
6 wrtpkseveral
7 alsomnbvcxfr
8 cxzanimalrzw

Write them here.

always
____
____
____
____
____
____
____

2 Now write each word under the correct heading.

Words that begin with *al*	Words that end with *al*
1 always	1 __________
2 __________	2 __________
3 __________	3 __________
4 __________	4 __________

3 Write the words in alphabetical order.

Words that begin with *al*

1 __________ 2 __________ 3 __________ 4 __________

Words that end with *al*

1 __________ 2 __________ 3 __________ 4 __________

Writing

1 Read about Lizzie's visit to the dentist. Fill in the missing words.

One day, my tooth hurt. My mum telephoned the dentist. On the way to the dentist, I felt very nervous.

When we arrived, we waited in a room. There were some books to read.

Soon it was my turn. I walked into the dentist's room. The dentist was wearing some ______________________ on her hands. She wore a ___________ on her face.

The dentist told me to sit in a big chair. The chair went up and down. Then the dentist turned on a bright ___________ . I opened my mouth. She looked in my mouth with a small ___________ . She saw a small hole in one tooth.

She gave me an ___________ . It made my mouth feel strange. After this, she used a ___________ to clean the hole in my tooth. She filled the hole and asked me to wash my mouth with pink water.

I went home with my mum. On the way home, my mouth felt funny. I like my dentist. She's nice!

2 Write about a visit you have made to the dentist.
Use Lizzie's account to help you.
Try to make it interesting.

Unit 18

Comprehension

1 **Read Language Book 4, pages 150–151 again.**

2 **Write *T* if the statement is true.**
Write *F* if the statement is false.

A friend is someone who:

1 forgives you when you are unkind. T
2 never smiles at you. ____
3 forgets you. ____
4 always respects you. ____
5 always remembers you. ____
6 calls you names. ____
7 is unkind to you. ____
8 includes you in games. ____
9 won't let you play with them. ____
10 encourages you when you are sad. ____
11 laughs at you when you are hurt. ____
12 discusses secret things with you. ____
13 never talks to you. ____
14 never hurts you. ____

Vocabulary

Words that **rhyme** contain the **same sound**.
Sometimes the words contain the **same letter pattern**: f**ace** pl**ace**
Sometimes the letter patterns are **different**: ins**ide** cr**ied**

1 Make some rhyming words. Write the new words you make.

1 Change the *f* in *fight* to *r*, *l*, *n* and *br*.

right ______ light ______ night ______ bright ______

2 Change the *l* in *look* to *b*, *c*, *t* and *h*.

______ ______ ______ ______

3 Change the *r* in *round* to *s*, *f*, *gr* and *ar*.

______ ______ ______ ______

4 Change the *c* in *care* to *sh*, *sc*, *st* and *squ*.

______ ______ ______ ______

2 Say the words. Match the pairs of rhyming words. Write the words.

1 fair	c		a try	fair pear
2 gate	___		b rude	______
3 high	___		c pear	______
4 said	___		d verse	______
5 food	___		e eight	______
6 nurse	___		f door	______
7 home	___		g head	______
8 more	___		h comb	______

Language building

Remember!
A **possessive pronoun** shows who **owns** something.
I have a computer. The computer is **mine**.

Possessive pronouns

mine   yours   his   hers   ours   theirs

1 Underline the possessive pronoun in each of these sentences.

1 This pen is mine.
2 Ben and Sam looked at Tom and Sarah's picture, but they liked theirs best.
3 'Is this coat yours?' Anna asked.
4 We made a lovely model – ours was the best in the class.
5 'This is hers,' the boy said. He picked up the book and pointed to Amy.
6 'Whose car is this? Is it his?' asked the police officer.

2 Replace the underlined words with possessive pronouns.

1 Your coat is newer than my coat (__mine__).
2 I have lost my pen. May I use your pen (__________)?
3 The girl can't find her bag. Is that her bag (__________) on the stool?
4 Tom picked up the muddy shoes – they were his shoes (__________).
5 'You can't have the ball. It's our ball (__________)!' shouted Mark and Millie.
6 The two children wanted some new toys. Their toys (__________) were broken.

Grammar

1 Find the right endings.

1 A nurse is __d__ a someone who works in an office.

2 An actor is ____ b someone who hunts wild animals illegally.

3 A secretary is ____ c someone who teaches at a university.

4 A poacher is ____ d someone who looks after patients in a hospital.

5 A professor is ____ e someone who performs on TV, in films or in the theatre.

2 Put the words in each sentence in the correct order.

1 who scuba someone swims A underwater. diver is

____

2 is who A controls football referee match. a someone

____

3 is who good An sport. athlete at someone is

____

4 clothes. someone is who A makes tailor

____

5 builds is engineer who An machines. someone

____

3 Complete the sentences.

1 A reporter is someone who ______________________________

2 A football fan ______________________________

3 A waiter ______________________________

4 Meet the Jolly family!

Andy Mrs Jolly Grandpa Grandma Mr Jolly Lucy

I'm good at making cakes.

I enjoy telling stories.

I love my family.

I work very hard as a doctor.

I'm interested in animals.

I love playing football.

Complete the sentences.

1 Andy is someone who ______________________________

2 Mrs Jolly ______________________________

3 Grandpa ______________________________

4 Grandma ______________________________

5 Mr Jolly ______________________________

6 Lucy ______________________________

5 Write about three people in your own family.

1 ______________________________

2 ______________________________

3 ______________________________

Spelling

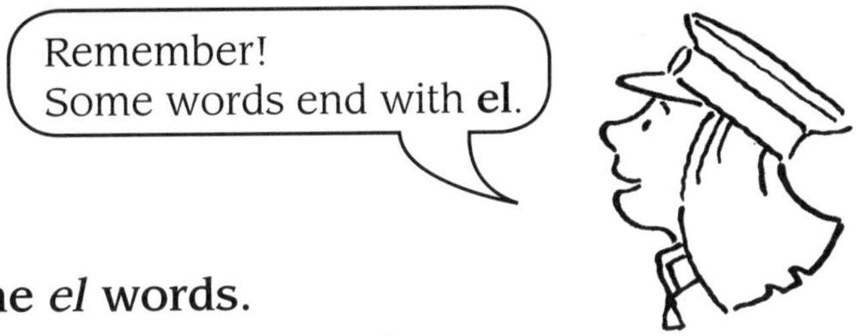

1 Make some *el* words.

cam, parc, jew, tow, hot → el →

1 camel
2 ______
3 ______
4 ______
5 ______

vow, lab, trav, tunn, squirr → el →

6 ______
7 ______
8 ______
9 ______
10 ______

2 Write the correct word under each picture.

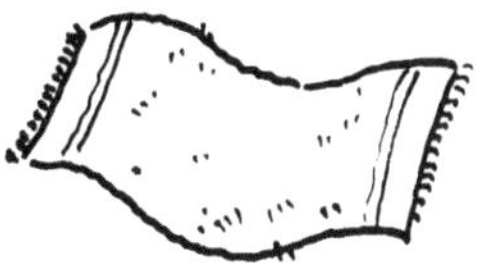

1 ______

2 ______

3 ______

4 ______

5 ______

6 ______

7 ______

8 ______

______

______

Writing

Matthew is writing an **acrostic poem**.
He is using the letters in his name.
He has written some adjectives.
He thinks they describe him.
He used a dictionary to help him find the words.

musical amazing handsome wonderful tall tidy exciting

1 **Help Matthew to complete his acrostic poem.**
Make the first letter of each line a different colour.

M usical

A ____________

T ____________

T ____________

H ____________

E ____________

W ____________

2 Write an acrostic poem. Use the letters in your name. If possible, use a dictionary to help you.

h l n w e j k o q s a c

t z p r b f g u y m x

Check-up 4

1 Complete each sentence with *just* or *yet*.

1  Haven't you done your homework __________ ?

2  Look! I have __________ found this gold coin.

3  Sam has not finished his lunch __________ .

4  Has Grandma found her glasses __________ ?

5  The fishermen have __________ caught a shark.

6  Dad has __________ given me this book to read.

2 Complete each sentence with *What a*, *What an* or *What*.

1  ____________________ beautiful butterfly!

2  ____________________ funny clowns!

3  ____________________ extraordinary hat!

4  ____________________ delicious food!

5  ____________________ interesting book!

6  ____________________ terrible weather!

3 **Make suggestions beginning with *How about* or *What about*.**

1 Shall we go to town? How about going to town?

2 Shall we go to a museum? ____________

3 Let's see a film! ____________

4 I'd like to walk by the river. ____________

5 Let's eat Chinese food! ____________

4 **Complete each sentence using a verb ending in *ing*.**

1 Harry loves ____________

2 Susie enjoys ____________

3 Paul is very good at ____________

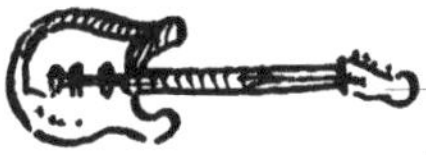

4 Jenny is interested in ____________

5 The children like ____________

6 Grandpa enjoys ____________

5 **Complete each sentence using a word from each box.**

works makes
looks after flies

hospital school restaurant
office sheep clothes planes

1 A nurse is someone who works in a ____________

2 A pilot ____________

3 A shepherd ____________

4 A waiter ____________

5 A teacher ____________

6 A tailor ____________

7 A secretary ____________

Final Check-up

1 Write questions to match the answers.

1 What ____________________ ? I heard a loud noise.
2 Where ____________________ ? He saw a cat on the roof.
3 How many ____________________ ? She had six presents.
4 How ____________________ ? They went to town by car.
5 When ____________________ ? We got the letter today.

2 What were the people doing when the photographer took the photos.

1  Billy ____________________

2  The twins ____________________

3  Dad ____________________

4  I ____________________

5  We ____________________

3 Complete each sentence with *Let's* or *Shall we*.

1 ____________________ go to the sports club!
2 ____________________ play tennis?
3 ____________________ go for a swim?
4 ____________________ have a cold drink!

4 Write questions to match the answers.

1 How ______________________________ to the airport?
They'll go by taxi.

2 What ______________________________ ?
They'll take their suitcases.

3 How many ______________________________ ?
They'll have five.

4 ______________________________ ?
Yes, their luggage will be heavy.

5 How long ______________________________ ?
The flight will last two hours.

6 Who ______________________________ ?
Their uncle will meet them.

5 Complete the sentences using words from the box.

anything	nothing	somebody	nobody

1  There is ______________________________

2  There is ______________________________

3  Is there ______________________________ ?

4  There is ______________________________

6 Write questions beginning with *Would you like*.

1  ______________________________

2  ______________________________

3  ______________________________

4  ______________________________

7 Match the beginning of each sentence with the correct ending.

1 If you go to Egypt, d
2 If Harry works hard, ____
3 If we get a cat, ____
4 I'll buy some flowers ____
5 They won't go to the beach ____
6 Mum will make a cake ____

a if I go to the market.
b if she has time.
c if it is raining.
d you'll see the pyramids.
e it will catch rats and mice.
f he'll pass his exams.

8 Complete each sentence with a word from each box.

have	heard won been
has	seen read played

1 Have you ever been to Australia?
2 The football team ____ never ____ a match.
3 I ____ never ____ an eagle.
4 ____ Peter ever ____ basketball?
5 ____ you ever ____ this book?
6 We ____ never ____ this song before.

9 **Write the questions for these answers. Use the words in the box.**

Which	How	What	How much
Why	When	How many	Where

1 ______________________________

Polar bears live in the Arctic.

2 ______________________________

Pandas eat bamboo.

3 ______________________________

An Indian elephant has smaller ears.

4 ______________________________

He went to Africa to see the lions.

5 ______________________________

He saw lots of lions.

6 ______________________________

He travelled by road.

7 ______________________________

Mr and Mrs Pitt will go to Mexico next year.

8 ______________________________

They have lots of money.

10 **Complete the story with the verbs in the box.**
Be careful to use the right tenses.
Make sure you use all the verbs.

ask	be	can	catch	come	feel	hear
laugh	look	make	reply	run	say	see
smile	stand	start	stop	think	walk	watch

Something exciting happened to Tom last week. While he ________________ home from school, he ________________ a big group of people. They ________________ outside a shop. It ________________ a jewellery shop. Suddenly a man ________________ out of the shop. He ________________ quickly to the right and the left and then ________________ as fast as he ________________ down the street. Tom ________________ a shout: "Stop, thief!"

"I ______________ good at ______________ ," ______________ Tom. "If I ______________ really fast, I ______________ him." He ______________ to run after the thief. The group of people ______________ loudly.

Then the thief ______________ running. Tom ______________ very surprised. "I ______________ an actor," the man ______________ . "We ______________ a film" Tom ______________ a bit silly but the actor ______________ at him. "Have you ever ______________ in a film?" he ______________ ." No," ______________ Tom. "Well," ______________ the actor, "you ______________ in one now! If you ______________ TV next Saturday, you ______________ in the programme!"

Macmillan Education
Between Towns Road, Oxford OX4 3PP
A division of Macmillan Publishers Limited
Companies and representatives throughout the world

ISBN 978-1-4050-8127-6

First published 2006

Designed by Jeffrey Tabberner
Layout by Chad Young
Illustrated by David Mostyn
Cover design by Oliver Design

Printed and bound in Malaysia

2014 2013 2012
10 9 8